Advanced Composition
for ESL Students

ISBN: 0-89089-560-0
LCCN: 2004113253

Carolina Academic Press
700 Kent Street
Durham, North Carolina 27701
Telephone (919) 489-7486
Fax (919) 493-5668
E-mail: cap@cap-press.com
www.cap-press.com

Advanced Composition for ESL Students

Bryan Ryan

Academic Dean
Wake Technical Community College

Carolina Academic Press
Durham, North Carolina

Contents

Preface vi

Chapter 1—The Building Blocks of Writing 1

Chapter 2—Paragraph Development 18

Chapter 3—Narrative Writing 28

Chapter 4—Essay Development: Body Paragraphs 44

Chapter 5—Essay Development: Introductions and Conclusions 54

Chapter 6—Process Writing 65

Chapter 7—Description 84

Chapter 8—Comparison and Contrast 106

Chapter 9—Evaluation 129

Chapter 10—Problem and Solution 150

Chapter 11—Cause and Effect 162

Chapter 12—The Research Paper 179

Extras 190

Index 214

Preface

Advanced Composition for ESL Students involves students in building a practical understanding of written communication—its audiences, purposes, and forms. They will learn and use a simple, yet effective process to improve their writing and their attitude toward it. They will extend their knowledge of the language by becoming familiar with the expectations of academic and other types of formal writing, especially at the college/university level and beyond.

As it leads students through the writing process, this textbook will also engage them in the kind of active learning expected in American schools—an educational approach that requires students to take responsibility for their own learning, to exercise critical thinking, to work cooperatively with peers, and to apply their new knowledge beyond the classroom.

As a composition textbook, *Advanced Composition for ESL Students* guides students in using traditional aids available to writers—reference books, handbooks, and library resources. It also introduces ESL writers to tools available through new media, such as the Internet. Along with its main focus, the book integrates reading, speaking, and grammar activities to emphasize their importance in good written communication.

The material that follows is designed to support teachers and students working together in a traditional classroom environment. It also includes activities that blend traditional instruction with learning at a distance. Each chapter is organized to lead students through the learning process by engaging, exploring, explaining, exercising/evaluating, and extending. With its detailed instructions, templates, review sheets, and appendices, *Advanced Composition for ESL Students* will serve students long after they leave the classroom.

Acknowledgments

I have had the great pleasure of working with students from over 70 different countries and cultures. Their feedback in the classroom about what works and what doesn't has provided me direction in teaching and in writing this book. I owe a great deal to my colleagues in the EFL Department at Wake Technical Community College in Raleigh, N.C. They have all shared their insights and their passion for teaching. Thanks go to colleagues in other departments at Wake Tech, especially in English and the Writing Center, for feedback about what makes EFL/ESL students successful in mainstream courses. I have also had the benefit of collaborating with peers from other institutions, notably Edith Allen and Diane Bryson from Duke University. Diane's review of the manuscript was especially helpful. Finally, my deepest appreciation goes to my most supportive readers, Sue, Sami, and Sunni Ryan.

Chapter 1—The Building Blocks of Writing

This chapter provides a brief review of the elements of writing—from letters of the alphabet through sentences. Students who need a more detailed review of these elements should consult one of the many ESL grammar textbooks or handbooks available.

1.1 Engage—Getting to Know Your Classmates

The purpose of this activity is for you to become acquainted with your classmates—your peers. You are all going to be working together for the next several weeks toward improving your writing skills, so there will be many chances to cooperate and collaborate. "You are all in the same boat," as Americans say, so you might as well get to know one another.

1. You are going to be collecting five different types of information on each of your classmates. To start, take out a sheet of paper and mark off five columns. The columns will contain the information indicated in Table 1.1, so you will want to make the columns wide enough for the information to fit. If every student is from the same country, use region, city, or some other location category instead. If all of the students are in the same program, use hobbies or other interests.

Table 1.1—Classmate Information

Last name (family name/ surname)	First name (given name)	Country of origin and continent	Major or career	Contact info*

*For contact information, you can use an e-mail address or a phone number. If a classmate does not want to share this information, you should respect her/his privacy. If you do not have e-mail, you should look into one of the many free Web-based e-mail providers. Classmates can show you how to set up an account, or you can use a search engine to find "free e-mail."

2. Collect this information on all of your classmates. Walk around the room and ask politely for the information. Take this opportunity to practice your conversation and question-asking skills. (30-40 minutes)

For example:

"Hello. I'm Bryan Ryan. What is your name? Is that your family name? Where are you from? What are you studying here at the college? Would you mind sharing your e-mail address with me? Thank you. It's a pleasure to meet you."

OR

"Hi. My name is Bryan Ryan. And you are...? It's nice to meet you. Could you spell your name for me? Thanks. Where are your from? Is that in Asia? What is your major? Really? What kind of job can you get with that major? Could I have your e-mail address? Thanks."

Don't forget to include your own information on your list.

3. After you have collected all of the information, sort it by three different characteristics. Make three separate lists. Organize each list alphabetically by the given characteristic. (20-30 minutes)

First List: Arrange alphabetically by last names. (See Table 1.2.)

Table 1.2—Names

Last name	First name	Country of origin and continent	Major or career	Contact info
Andersen	Hans	Denmark, Europe	Writer	andersonhc @mailprovider.net
...				
Zola	Emile	France, Europe	Writer	ezola@electricpost. fr

Second List: Arrange alphabetically by country of origin. (See Table 1.3.)

Table 1.3—Country of Origin

Country of origin	Last name	First name	Major or career	Contact info
Argentina, South America	Peron	Juan	Politician	peronj @mailprovider.net
...				
Zimbabwe, Africa	Nkomo	Joshua	Politician	jnkomo@cybermail.zb

Third List: Arrange alphabetically by major or career.   (See Table 1.4.)

Table 1.4—Major or Career

Major or career	Last name	First name	Country of origin and continent	Contact info
Aviation	Bleriot	Louis	France, Europe	channelcross @mailprovider.net
...				
Chemistry and physics	Curie	Marie	Poland, Europe	twonobels @cybermail.fr

1.2 Explore—General Reference Sources

One great thing about learning English in a group of international students is that you have the opportunity to learn about different people and their homelands. Even if you are studying in a group that has students from only one country, you still have an opportunity to learn more about the people and the regions or cities that they are from.

1. Look at your second list from the "Engage" activity, the list arranged by country of origin. Find the name of three countries that you know the least about. Using your own resources, library reference books (almanacs, atlases, or encyclopedias), or online sources, find out the following information about each of the countries.

Country name:

Location (continent and bordering countries):

Size:
Area—

Population—

Capital and other large cities:

Languages:

Religions:

Primary economic activities:

Current leader:

One interesting historical event:

2. Now choose one of the countries that you researched and write one paragraph (approximately 10 sentences or 100 words) about that country. Use the details that you found in the reference sources. Organize the details in whatever way you think makes the most sense. Write complete sentences. You will share your paragraph with a classmate from that country and then with your professor.

1.3 Explain—The Building Blocks of Writing

In order to write well, you need a strong understanding of the building blocks of writing. Real building blocks, though small, can be put together in rows to make walls, which can be put together to make rooms, which can be put together to make buildings, which can be put together to make cities. The same is true with the building blocks of writing. Small parts are put together to make larger parts that are put together to make even larger parts, and so on.

The English Alphabet—From Sound to Symbol

The English language uses an alphabet to capture the sounds of the spoken language in visual symbols. The basic idea of an alphabet is that one symbol (a letter) in the written language represents one sound in the spoken language.

With this in mind, a language should have as many letters as it has sounds. It should have. However, English has almost twice as many sounds as letters. There are about 45 sounds in spoken American English, but we use only 26 letters in written English.

abcdefghijklmnopqrstuvwxyz

The reason for the difference in number of sounds and letters is historical. English, like many European languages, has been greatly influenced by Latin, the common language of the ancient Romans. The English alphabet, also like those used by many European languages, was borrowed from the Roman alphabet. English speakers had to adapt this alphabet to fit all the sounds already in their spoken language. For this reason, some letters used in written English can represent more than one sound, and some sounds are represented by more than one letter.

The English Phonetic (Sound) System

Vowels

In making vowel sounds, you force air out of your lungs. This air moves through your windpipe (trachea) and through your voice box (larynx) in your throat, where it accompanies the vibration of your vocal cords. From there, the air moves through your mouth, passing over your tongue without anything stopping it. You can hold, or continue, these sounds for as long as you still have air in your lungs to force through your voice box across your tongue. When singers hold a note for a long time, they are holding a vowel sound.

There are about 15 vowel sounds in American English. An easy way to remember these sounds is to put them into simple key words. You can then use those key words to refer to the vowel sounds. For example:

H<u>e</u> w<u>i</u>ll s<u>ay</u>, "B<u>e</u>t th<u>a</u>t
g<u>ir</u>l w<u>a</u>s l<u>o</u>st.
C<u>a</u>ll h<u>o</u>me. C<u>ou</u>ld y<u>ou</u>
tr<u>y</u> n<u>ow</u>, b<u>oy</u>?"

As you can see, these 15 sounds are represented by 6 letters (**a e i o u y**), used alone or in combination with each other and with some vowel-loving consonants. (Look below for more on consonants.) The vowel-loving consonants are *y* and *w*. Combinations of letters show that English vowel sounds, especially American English vowel sounds, are not pure; that means they often have more than one sound.

Consonants

When you speak, you make consonant sounds by blocking or diverting the air used in speaking as it passes through your throat and mouth. There are many ways to block the air using the parts of your mouth—tongue, teeth, and lips—and sometimes parts of your throat. For some consonant sounds, you block and release air. These are called stops. For other consonant sounds, you restrict the air but do not stop it. These are called continuants. Continuants are like vowel sounds because they can be held for as long as air remains in your lungs.

Some stops and continuants are like vowels because they involve vibrations of the voice box. These sounds are called voiced sounds. Other stops and continuants are made without vibrating the voice box. These are called voiceless sounds. (See Table 1.5.)

Table 1.5—Consonants

	Stops	Continuants
Voiced	b, d, g, j	w, m, z, zh, n, v, l, ng, r, th (the), y
Voiceless	p, t, k, ch	f, s, sh, th (theater), h, wh

Some languages require that each consonant sound be paired with a vowel sound to form a simple syllable (see Syllables below). English allows some consonant sounds to be combined with other consonant sounds in groups of two or three or sometimes even four. These combinations are called blends. Common blends include bl, br, cl, cr, fl, fr, gl, gr, pl, pr, sc, sk, sl, sm, sn, sp, st, sw, tr, thr, scr, spl, spr, and str.

Syllables—Capturing Rhythm and Meaning

Spoken English, like all languages, has its own musical qualities. It uses rhythm—like the beats of a drum—and intonation—the tones (low, middle, and high)—to organize sounds and differentiate between them, as well as to carry meaning. Each time you clap your hands, snap your fingers, or tap your toes, you are creating a beat, and the relationship between the beats is the rhythm. Each individual vowel sound in spoken English falls on one beat. Sometimes these vowel sounds stand alone on the beat, and sometimes they are joined on the beat by one or more consonant sounds.

When spoken on a single beat, each vowel sound and the consonant sounds linked to it form a syllable. In other words, when you use a vowel sound or combine a vowel sound with consonants and speak them together on a single beat, you are creating a syllable. In speaking, a syllable is the smallest unit of rhythm. When you listen to or speak English, you should be able to hear syllables rather easily.

It is more difficult to see syllables in written English than to hear them in spoken English. The only thing that you can be sure of is that the first syllable of a word begins at the beginning of the word and the last syllable ends at the end of the word. Your best bet is to use your knowledge of the sounds of English to divide the vowel sounds of words into syllables between beats—usually between two distinct vowel sounds or two distinct consonant sounds. Sometimes you may find that a syllable stands alone if a distinct vowel is not linked any neighboring sounds.

Words

A word consists of one or more syllables used together to communicate meaning or to perform a grammatical function. In writing, words are separated by a space from other words. There are two main types of words in English, content words and function words.

Content Words

Content words carry the main meaning in English sentences. They can also be changed to include different elements of meaning.

Verbs   Adverbs   Nouns   Adjectives

Verbs describe actions or states of being (existence and internal processes). Verbs change their form to express number (singular or plural) and to express time frame (past, present, or future), focus (before, during, or after), and action (habitual, finished, or unfinished).

Actions

Examples of frequently used action verbs:

ask	drink	lie	sing	tell
beat	eat	live	sit	thank
become	fall	look	sleep	try
begin	find	make	speak	turn
bite	fly	open	stand	use
bring	get	put	stay	wait
call	give	rain	stop	wake
come	go	read	swim	walk
cry	keep	run	take	wish
do	let	say	talk	write

States of Being

Examples of frequently used stative verbs:

be	have	mean	see	understand
believe	hear	need	seem	want
belong	know	own	smell	
dislike	like	prefer	taste	
hate	love	remember	think	

(For more information about verbs, see Chapter 3—"Narrative Writing," and the "Extra" chapter at the end of the book.)

Adverbs give more information about (or modify) verbs, adjectives, or other adverbs. Adverbs can also modify clauses or whole sentences. They usually provide information that answers the questions when, where, how, how much, or how often. Some adverbs change their form to express comparative relationships and superlative relationships (-er, -est, more, or most).

Adverbs typically come after the verb that they modify. (A specific adverb may be separated from the verb it modifies by another adverb or by phrases that function as adverbs.) However, adverbs that describe HOW OFTEN usually come before the verb that they modify.

Adverbs that modify adjectives and other adverbs come before the words that they modify. Adverbs that modify clauses or sentences can be found at the beginning or end of the clause or sentence.

Examples of adverbs:

WHEN	WHERE	HOW	HOW MUCH	HOW OFTEN
afterwards	away	clockwise	almost	always
annually	back	easily	barely	usually
daily	down	fast	entirely	generally
late	eastward	happily	just	regularly
meanwhile	forward	lazily	quite	often
monthly	homeward	logically	really	frequently
now	northward	nowhere	relatively	sometimes
today	sideways	quickly	scarcely	occasionally
tomorrow	southward	simply	too	seldom
weekly	up	smoothly	very	rarely
yesterday	westward	studiously	virtually	never

(For more on adverbs, see the "Extra" chapter at the end of the book.)

Nouns are people, places, things, and concepts. Nouns can be either common (a general example—man, city, car, religion) or proper (the specific name of the example—Joe Wilson, Chicago, Ford Mustang, Buddhism). Nouns can be count or noncount. Count nouns can change their form to express singular (one) or plural (more than one). Noncount nouns do not typically change their form. They do not really express singular or plural; they capture a collective feel.

Table 1.6 provides some examples of nouns.

Table 1.6—Nouns

	Common Nouns	**Proper Nouns**
Count Nouns	person (people) lake(s) drink(s) philosophy (-ies)	American(s) Great Lake(s) Dr. Bob's Root Beer(s) Marxism*
Noncount Nouns	coffee sugar intelligence news	Morning Moment Coffee Sweet Crystals Sugar National Intelligence MSD News

*Proper nouns are often so specific that they do not have a plural.

(For more on nouns, see the "Extra" chapter at the end of the book.)

Adjectives describe nouns. Adjectives typically come before the noun that they describe. Adjectives can change their form to express comparative and superlative relationships (-er, -est, more, or most). Adjectives can provide several different types of information about nouns. For example:

Evaluation—amazing, boring, beautiful, ugly, delicious, disgusting ...
Size—big, immense, tall, tiny, wide ...
Age—ancient, futuristic, new, nineteenth-century, old ...
Shape—oval, pointed, round, square, triangular ...
Condition—broken, cracked, torn, whole ...
Action—bouncing, falling, oscillating, pulsating ...
Color—black, blue, green, orange, red, turquoise, white, yellow ...
Origin—African, Celtic, Hispanic, Swiss, Texan, Vietnamese ...
Ideology—Buddhist, communist, democratic, Muslim ...
Material—aluminum, chocolate, cotton, plastic, wooden ...

Function Words

Function words are important in completing the structure of sentences (see below). They connect words and create a finished, smoothly flowing sentence. They also carry some meaning, though subtle shades of meaning.

Function words include determiners, prepositions, pronouns, and conjunctions. We will explore function words through exercises in later chapters.

Phrases

A phrase is a group of words. Together these words serve a common grammatical purpose. For example, a verb phrase is a group of words that function together as a verb; an adverb phrase is a group of words that function together as an adverb. Noun and adjective phrases work the same way. The additional words in each type of phrase help add detail to the content words. Also, because adverbs describe verbs and adjectives describe nouns, adverb phrases are often parts of verb phrases and adjective phrases are often parts of noun phrases.

Another type of common phrase is the prepositional phrase. A prepositional phrase = preposition + a noun phrase. (See the "Extra" chapter for a list of common prepositions.) Prepositional phrases are often used like adjectives to describe nouns or like adverbs to modify verbs.

The collector bought the book <u>with the black leather cover</u>. (The phrase functions as an adjective describing *book*.)

The firefighters arrived <u>in the nick of time</u>. (The phrase functions as an adverb describing when the firefighters arrived.)

Sentences

Letters, syllables, words, and phrases are all progressively larger parts of written communication. Letters represent individual sounds. We put these letters together to make syllables. Syllables represent individual beats and also carry pieces of meaning. We put syllables together to make words. Words express meaning and grammatical function. Groups of words that together have a similar function are phrases. With each level of development, we add more meaning. Even so, none of these components offers a completed unit of meaning and none can stand alone grammatically.

A sentence is the smallest complete unit of meaning and smallest collection of words (or phrases) that can stand alone grammatically. Sentences express statements, questions, and commands. They may be simple, compound, or complex. (See the "Extra" chapter for more about sentence types.)

Characteristics of a Complete Sentence

A complete sentence:

1. Has a verb with a time frame—A complete sentence must contain a verb. However, because there are action words that are not really verbs, it is important that the verb in each sentence clearly express one of the four time frames: past, present, future, or always. (See Chapter 3 for an overview of the different time frames.)

Fit requirements
... found ... (past)
... are ... (present)
... have written ... (present)
... will be swimming ... (future)

Do not fit requirements
... to find ... (time frame not clear)
... be ... (time frame not clear)
... written ... (time frame not clear)
... swimming ... (time frame not clear)

2. Has a subject—A complete sentence must contain a subject. A subject is the noun or noun substitute that does the action of the verb or carries the state of being. In addition to nouns, verbals—gerunds (action words in "-ing" form) and infinitives (action words in the "to verb" form)—can serve as sentence subjects. Subject pronouns also function as subjects. These are *I, you, he, she, it, we, they*. Note: In commands (the imperative form), the subject is understood to be *you*, so commands fit the requirement of having a subject.

3. Follows a standard order—The usual order of the elements of a complete sentence are:

SUBJECT + VERB + {OBJECT or COMPLEMENT}   { } = not always necessary

The VERB and the elements that follow it are often called the PREDICATE.

In sentences with more detail, the usual order of sentence elements is (reading down):

SUBJECT	I	Judy	Members
VERB	drove	read	elected
Indirect Object	|	the children	|
Direct Object	my car	the book	Frank
Object Complements	|	|	president
Verb Complements of Place	to the store	|	at the last meeting.
Verb Complements of Time	after dinner.	during the trip.	

OR

SUBJECT	Bob Shocker	The stew
VERB (stative)	is	smells
Subject Complements	the new chief information officer.	delicious.

4. Is not dependent—Some groups of words that look like a complete sentence—because they have a verb with a time frame, a subject, and standard word order—are actually dependent on other words to complete their meaning and stand alone grammatically. These groups of words are called **dependent clauses**. Dependent clauses begin with words called subordinating conjunctions, and it is these function words that make independent clauses into dependent clauses. Subordinating conjunctions show relationships of time, cause and effect, contrast, and condition.

TIME	CAUSE and EFFECT	CONTRAST	CONDITION
after	because	although	even if
as	in order that	even though	if
as soon as	since (= because)	though	in the event that
before	so	whereas	provided that
by the time that	so that	while (= whereas)	unless
since			whether or not
until			
when			
whenever			
while			

In order for a sentence with a dependent clause to be complete, it must be connected with an **independent clause**, another group of words that meets the requirements of a complete sentence. This independent clause must have a subject and a verb that indicates the time frame.

5. Has appropriate punctuation—A complete sentence begins with a capital letter (A, B, C ... Z) and ends with a full stop (. ? !).

See the "Extra" chapter at the end of the book for information on simple, compound, and complex sentences.

1.4 Exercise / Evaluate

Exercise 1: Finding Vowel Sounds

Under each of the words in Tables 1.7 through 1.10, list six other words that share the same vowel sound.

Table 1.7—Front Vowels

he	will	say	bet	that
bean	bit	bait	less	lab

Table 1.8—Central Vowels

girl	was	lost
worm	cut	hop

Table 1.9—Back Vowels

call	home	could	you
caught	note	put	new

Table 1.10—Blended Vowels (Diphthongs)

try	now	boy
find	doubt	oil

Exercise 2: Word Form Endings

For each of the following word form endings, find 3 more words of the same type that share the same ending. Check in your dictionary to ensure that each word you find is the appropriate word form. For examples of more word form endings, see the "Extra" section at the end of the book.

<u>Verb Endings</u>

-ate: originate

-ceive: deceive

-fer: transfer

-ify: glorify

-ize: sanitize

-uct: conduct

<u>Adverb Endings</u>

-ly: slowly

-ward: upward

<u>Noun Endings</u>

-acy: bureaucracy

-ance: importance

-er: teacher

-ion: nation

-ment: retirement

-ness: happiness

<u>Adjective Endings</u>

-able: capable

-al: original

-ent: recent

-ful: successful

-less: helpless

-ous: delicious

Exercise 3: Counting Syllables

Counting syllables in words can be important when making the comparative and superlative forms of adverbs and adjectives. (For more on comparatives and superlatives, see Chapters 8 and 9.) Count the syllables in the following adverbs and adjectives. Write the number (#) next to the regular form. If the regular form has one syllable, or two syllables AND ends with a -*y* (not -*ly*) or -*le*, you can make the comparative by adding -*er* and the superlative by adding -*est* (change the final -*y* to an *i*). If the regular form has two or more syllables, you should use "more" to make the comparative and "most" to make the superlative.

Regular form	# of syllables	Comparative	Superlative
loud	1	louder	loudest
important	3	more important	most important

contentious

difficult

happy

lazy

northward

secretively

significant

small

Exercise 4: Finding the Main Verb of a Sentence

Read each sentence carefully. Find the main verb of the sentence. There is only one main verb. There should be a letter (A, B, C, or D) directly in front of this main verb. Circle the letter that comes directly in front of the main verb.

1. The United States (A) has the largest and most technologically (B) advanced economy in the world, (C) giving it a great (D) deal of economic power.

2. Although it (A) was at one time the strongest (B) manufacturing country in the world, it now (B) employs more people in managerial and technical professions—(C) including computer (D) programming—than in traditional industries.

3. Because it (A) has a free-market economy, the people who (B) purchase goods (C) have great influence on how the economy (D) functions.

4. Even so, the federal (A) government in Washington, D.C., (B) and each of the fifty state governments, (C) take action to (D) promote stability and growth.

5. The United States (A) exports manufactured goods, consumer (B) products, natural resources, and agricultural goods (C) to trade partners such as Canada, Mexico, (D) Japan, and the United Kingdom.

6. The economy (A) regularly (B) experiences cycles of rapid growth and (C) slow growth as world events and domestic policy (D) influence the various economic sectors.

7. The nation's numerous (A) banking centers and commodities and stock (B) exchanges (C) make it a leading financial (D) center in the world.

8. The (A) influence of the American (B) economy on the (C) rest of the world (D) is increasing.

9. Even so, (A) domestic issues, (B) including national and personal debt, (C) will continue (D) to present challenges for the American people over the next decade.

10. The nation's (A) money (B) is the (C) U.S. (D) dollar.

Exercise 5: Identifying Complete Sentences

Review the requirements of a complete sentence. Then, read each group of words below carefully. Decide if each is a complete sentence (YES) or not a complete sentence (NO), and then explain why.

1. The United States of America is one of the largest countries in the world.

2. The third largest country in the world in both area and population.

3. The area of the United States is 9.6 million square kilometers.

4. On the north by Canada and on the south by Mexico.

5. The U.S.A. stretches from the Atlantic Ocean in the east to the Pacific Ocean in the west.

6. Approximately 290 million people live in the United States.

7. Many ethnic groups are represented in the United States, but the majority of the population (77 percent) is white, primarily of European descent.

8. Minority groups include African-Americans (13 percent), Native Americans (1.5 percent), and Asians or Pacific Islanders (4.5 percent).

9. Many Americans coming from Spanish-speaking countries in Central and South America, the Caribbean, and Spain.

10. The number of Asians is growing faster than that of any other group.

1.5 Extend

Pulling It All Together—Together with your classmates, collect all your paragraphs about countries from the Explore activity above. Find out if all of the home countries of the students have been described. If not, work together in groups to complete summaries on the missing countries. When you have completed all of the summaries, bring them together into a class almanac. Use a word processor to make your almanac neat and readable. Add flags and maps available from clip art or from online sources that provide images in the public domain. Publish your almanac for others to read, either in a hard-copy form or on a Web site (if such resources are available to you).

Beyond the Classroom—Writing poses many challenges for international students. You will be more successful if you get a lot of practice and feedback both inside and outside the classroom. If you have not done so already, find out what kind of resources your college or university offers to help writers. Are there special resources in the library? Does your school have a writing center or lab? Are tutors available to help writers?

Also, the Internet now has many online writing centers (or online writing labs—OWLs). These Web sites offer explanations of concepts associated with writing, and they have exercises for practicing what you have learned. You can use your favorite search engine to find a list of "online writing centers" or "online writing labs."

Using Technology—You can get an idea of how words are used in typical English writing by trying this activity. It requires a computer with a word processor and an Internet connection. Do the following:

1. Find an online magazine. There are many online news and popular magazines. Some online portals/search engines also offer news.

2. Choose an interesting article.

3. Select about 100 words (one or two paragraphs), copy them, and paste them into a word processor document.

4. Use your Replace feature (usually under the Edit menu) to replace all spaces with returns (or paragraph marks). This will put every word on its own line, making a list.

5. Select all of the words and use your Sort feature to sort the words alphabetically. Now you have a list of alphabetized words.

6. Observe the list. Which words are repeated most often? Which words are content words? Are they verbs, adverbs, nouns, or adjectives? Which words are function words? Are there more content words or more function words? What else do you notice?

Chapter 2—Paragraph Development

This chapter focuses on the six essential elements of good paragraphs and gives a step by step approach to writing a good paragraph.

2.1 Engage—Organizing a Library

This activity introduces the concepts of classifying and organizing from general to specific. It also introduces the classification system that your library uses to organize its collection.

The activity is in two parts. The first part will involve classifying related concepts and then ordering them from general to specific. The second part will involve visiting the library to compare your classifications with the system used by the library. It may take two class meetings to complete. Or, one of the two parts may need to be done outside class as homework.

Forming Groups: Divide into groups by continent of origin. (If most students are from the same country, use regions or smaller classifications to form groups.) Use the continents individually—(1) Africa, (2) Asia, (3) Australia and Oceania, (4) Europe, (5) North and Central America, or (6) South America. Within each continent group, divide by country of origin. Students should choose a partner from outside their continent of origin— if possible—or from outside their country of origin. One group may need to have three people.

Part 1

a. In your group of two or three, look at the items in the columns below. On a separate sheet of paper, group items that are related into categories. For example, Hinduism is related to Religion. The Invention of Television is related to Technology. (Use 20 minutes.)

Alzheimer's Disease	Internet	Rock and Roll
Andes Mountains	Islam	Sciences
Arts	Korean	Shakespeare
Bach	Language	Sign Language for the Deaf
Buddhism	Law	Social Sciences
Business Ethics	Literature	Socrates
Calculus	Maps of Asia	Stock Markets
Cloning	Mathematics	Supreme Court of the USA
Community Colleges	Medicine	Swahili
Constitution of the USA	Music	Tahiti
Economics	Painting	Technology
Education	Philosophy	20th-Century English Poetry
Geography	Picasso	University Learning
Global Warming	Politics	World War II
History	Psychology	Writing
Immunizations	Religion	Yellowstone Park

b. Within each category, organize the items from top to bottom with general at the top and specific at the bottom. For example, you would organize Technology, Television, Cable Television in order from general to specific. (Use about 15 minutes.)

Part 2

a. Visit your library. Together with your partner, find out what classification system your library uses to organize its collection. You should discover that it uses (a) Dewey Decimal System, (b) the Library of Congress System, or (c) another system. Ask the librarians if they have material explaining the classification system. (Use about 10 minutes.)

b. Use the overview of the classification scheme, the subject search section of the library catalog, and direct exploration of the book stacks to find the classification code—numbers and/or letters—for each of the items on your list from #2 above. Write down the numbers and letters used to classify each topic next to that item on your list. If you cannot find the classification code for any of the items on you list, ask a librarian for assistance. Librarians usually have a book with classification codes for every subject. (Use about 45 minutes.)

c. Compare the way you classified the items in Part 1 of this activity to the way the library classifies them. What are the similarities? What are the differences? Write a paragraph of 50 to 100 words to explain how the library's classification system works and why it is useful to library patrons. (Use 15 minutes.)

2.2 Explore—Classification Schemes

Classification is an extremely useful tool. It allows people to bring order to a very complex world by grouping related items together (using similarities). Once they are grouped, it is also easier to see general to specific relationships. **Genealogy** groups people together by their family relationships. These family relationships have been very important throughout history, especially as they relate to kings and queens and other leaders. **Taxonomy** names and classifies living things. Biologists and others use taxonomy to better understand the relationships between organisms. The **departments** of a department store are actually categories used by the store to organize the thousands of things it has to sell. These departments make it easier for customers to find what they need. There are many other **classification schemes**.

Activity

1. Group the items in each of the following word lists into four groups based on their similarities. Give each group a title that names the category. Put related categories into larger categories and give these larger categories a name. For example, Beijing and Shanghai go together in a category called China; Tokyo and Osaka go together in a category called Japan; and China and Japan go together in a category called Asia.

List 1	List 2	List 3
bikinis	buffalo	biology
blouses	daffodil	chemistry
bowls	elephant	dentistry
dress shirts	ginkgo	economics
dresses	lily	graphic design
lamps	maple	history
microwave	oak	mathematics
neckties	pine	medicine
pots and pans	rose	painting
purses	salmon	pharmacy
recliner	shark	photography
rugs	sunfish	physics
silverware	tiger	political science
sofa	tulip	radiology
suits	tuna	sculpture
work boots	whale	sociology

2. Find another classification scheme used to help simplify your daily life. Think about the food people eat, the entertainment they enjoy, the activities that they do. List a few of the major categories used in this scheme and give a few examples of items that fit in each category.

2.3 Explain—Paragraph Structure

When writers need more than a word, phrase, or sentence to explore an idea, or address a question or problem, they need to develop a response in greater detail. After the sentence, the next level of organized writing is the **paragraph**. A paragraph allows a writer to explore a topic or develop a response to a question or problem that is neither too simple nor too complex. Even so, paragraphs can be linked together to address the most complex issues. This means that when writers learn to write good paragraphs, they are well on their way to writing whatever they desire.

The paragraph is the fundamental building block of good written communication. It is a microcosm. In other words, the paragraph contains all of the elements of longer writing— essays, chapters, books, multi-volume series—in a small space. In order to master these longer forms of writing, writers must first learn to develop a good paragraph.

Developing a Paragraph

You have already used paragraphs in your writing for this course, but now you are going to formally look at the paragraph to learn more about how to make paragraphs more effective.

Developing a good paragraph requires writers to know and use six elements:

Topic   This is the idea, question, or problem to be explored.
Focus—Because ideas can be complex, paragraphs have a focus to limit the idea to a manageable size. The focus makes general ideas more specific.
Support—This is the evidence used to explain, answer, or develop—to support—the focused topic.
Logic—The evidence used to support the focused topic should build according to accepted and expected forms of reasoning.
Unity—Each sentence in the paragraph must be connected to the focused topic. Evidence that does not directly support the focused topic must not be included.
Coherence—The evidence and the sentences that express it should flow smoothly from one to the next. Each sentence should be linked to the sentence before and after it.

How to Write a Paragraph

In order to write an effective paragraph, you can follow these steps:

1. Write a topic sentence

a. A topic sentence includes a topic (general idea, question, or problem to be explored) and the focus that limits the topic. Focusing tools (specific aspects) include:

time
place
number or sequence
category or characteristic
similarity or difference
quality (good, bad, or other)
cause or effect
problem or solution

b. Strong topic sentences place the topic in the subject position of the sentence. For this reason, strong topic sentences do not begin with "There is/are" or "It is/They are." For example, "Competitive badminton is very different from the backyard version." is better than "There are a lot of differences between competitive badminton and the backyard version."

c. Strong topic sentences are statements (never questions) that require further development. They are not obvious statements that can be completely explained in a single sentence. In other words, "Benjamin's shirt is blue" is not a good topic sentence because it does not require any development. "Benjamin dresses in a way that reflects his personality." is better because it needs to be explained.

2. (Optional) Write a sentence to define or clarify your topic sentence—You may need to add a definition, a description, details, or examples to make your topic sentence clear.

3. Write sentences to support or develop the topic sentence—You will need from one to several sentences to complete your exploration of the focused topic.

4. Write a concluding sentence—You may need a sentence to refer back to the topic sentence, to summarize, or to provide a transition to another paragraph.

Patterns of Development

The focus of paragraphs (or essays or research papers) gives direction to a writer about how to develop and organize the supporting details, essentially providing a pattern for the writer to follow. These patterns are called **rhetorical forms**. Below are the forms used most commonly.

Narration—Telling a story from beginning to end.
Process—Explaining step by step how something is done.
Classification and Division—Taking many things and grouping them together by type, or taking one thing and dividing it into its parts.
Description—Describing the characteristics of a subject.
Comparison and Contrast—Focusing on the similarities and/or differences of two or more subjects.
Evaluation—Judging a subject against a set of established standards or criteria.
Problem and Solution—Identifying and defining an issue and offering ways to address it.
Cause and Effect—Following how some events lead to others.

Related Structures

Coherence is a characteristic of good writing at the paragraph level and in longer writing. It means that the ideas and grammatical structures in a sentence are linked smoothly to the ideas and structures in sentences that come before and after. It also means that ideas and structures in a paragraph are linked smoothly to the ideas and structures in the paragraphs that come before and after.

Two ways to create coherence in your writing are by using transitions and by using repetition.

Transitions for Creating Coherence

Adding Information—also, and, furthermore, in addition, moreover, too
Comparing—likewise, similarly
Contrasting—but, even so, however, in contrast, nevertheless, nonetheless, on the other hand, still (= even so), yet
Concluding—in conclusion, in the end
Giving Examples—for example, for instance, in fact, namely
Showing Effect—as a result, consequently, hence, so, therefore, thus
Summarizing—in summary, to sum up

Using Repetition to Create Coherence

By repeating words, concepts, and grammatical structures in sentences and paragraphs, you can create connections between them. Good writers, speakers, and poets provide examples of the effective use of repetition.

President John F. Kennedy once said, "Ask not what your country can do for you. Ask what you can do for your country."

Martin Luther King wove together the many points of his famous speech delivered on the steps of the Lincoln Memorial in Washington, D.C., by beginning several of his paragraphs with "I have a dream..."

The American poet Robert Frost begins and ends his poem of reflection on life's choices, "The Road Not Taken," with the words "two roads diverged in a yellow wood."

Now that you are aware of the use of transitions and repetition to create coherence, look for these strategies in the things that you read, and incorporate them into your own writing.

2.4 Exercise / Evaluate

Exercise 1: Warm-up Writing

In a paragraph (10-12 sentences), explain to the reader the different types of degrees available from your college. Your audience is students who are preparing for higher education and those new to your college. Your purpose is to inform these prospective and new students about the opportunities available so that they can choose an appropriate degree. Introduce each type of degree and explain its basic requirements and purpose—the disciplines of study and the careers associated with each degree.

If you do not know much about the degrees offered at your college or you need more information, you may want to interview someone who has been there longer, or you may want to get more information from the advising and counseling resources at your school. You can also explain the kinds of diplomas or degrees available from high schools or universities in your home country.

One way to start is:
Quality Community College offers a variety of degrees to help prepare students for careers and for further study. The main degrees available are Associate in Applied Sciences (AAS), Associate in Arts (AA), and Associate in Sciences (AS). The AAS Degree...

Exercise 2: Skill/Structure Practice

A. Focusing topics. Remember, you read above about how to write a paragraph. After you choose a general topic, you need to use focusing tools to help make the topic more specific. The focusing tools are: (1) time; (2) place; (3) number or sequence; (4) category or characteristic; (5) similarity or difference; (6) quality (good, bad, or other); (7) cause or effect; and (8) problem or solution. For each of the following general topics, add specific examples of these focusing tools to make the topic more specific.

For example: bathrooms——> the differences between high-tech Japanese toilets and American toilets (focused on category [toilets], quality [high-tech], place [Japan and U.S.], time [implied present day], and difference).

colonialism—

crime—

drugs—

heroes—

homes—

Internet—

marriage—

smoking—

sports—

technology—

B. Writing topic sentences—Write a good topic sentence for each of the focused topics you have created above in Exercise 2A. See "How to Write a Paragraph" above for a reminder of the characteristics of a good topic sentence.

For example:

Because of their use of technology, Japanese toilets are quite different from American toilets, especially in terms of their efficient water use, their numerous comfort features, and their high cost.

C. Adding support. After you have established a focused topic and written your topic sentence, you need to include details to support your topic sentence. For the topic sentences written below, write two details that you could use to support the focused topic.

For example: North Carolina is beautiful in the autumn of the year.
a. The weather is cool and crisp with many sunny days.
b. The leaves of the trees turn vibrant colors: bright yellow, flaming orange, and deep red.

1. _____(My country)_____ has a rich culture.

2. Divorce is bad for children.

3. American families are different from those in my country.

4. Immigration benefits the United States.

5. This college/university is a good place to study.

6. Fast food poses a health risk.

7. Technology has made our lives easier.

8. English is an international language.

9. Television has a negative impact on society.

10. The European Union has similarities to the United States.

D. Maintaining unity. A paragraph should only contain details that support the focused topic. If it does, it has unity. Look at the groups of details below. Decide which detail does not fit with the others in each group. Circle the misplaced detail and explain why it does not fit.

1. red, orange, yellow, green, sky, blue, violet
2. grandfather, godfather, father, mother, sister, brother, granddaughter
3. Alps, Andes, Himalayas, Rockies, Sahara, Urals
4. dentists, doctors, lawyers, presidents, professors, psychiatrists

5. infidelity, laws that make divorce easy, marriage too young, single parenthood, work demands
6. Bangkok, Beijing, Kuala Lumpur, Seoul, Shanghai, Tokyo
7. emotions, height, lung capacity, stamina, strength, weight
8. CDs, DVDs, HDTV, Internet, JPEGs, newspapers
9. auto emissions, CFCs, deforestation, greenhouse gases, increased temperature, pollution
10. boating, camping, fishing, hiking, job training, walking

Exercise 3: Focused Writing Practice

This exercise will give you more practice writing a paragraph using classification and division. The classification and division pattern allows you to explore the relationship between general and specific things, by either grouping specific examples together within a common type, or by dividing a general item into its component parts. This type of writing is useful in many fields.

A. Writing a Paragraph. Explain the three most effective forms of transportation for getting around in your country. You may choose to focus on (1) getting around within cities, OR (2) getting around between cities. (Choose only one.) Your audience is a group of foreign travelers who need to get around during their visit to your country. Your purpose is to inform your audience about transportation so that they have an enjoyable and productive visit.

Write one paragraph that includes details on all three types of transportation. Make the paragraph as complete and well written as you can. Use details that will help your readers. Be sure to arrange your information logically, maintain unity, and build coherence.

For example,

Washington, D.C., has many attractions for tourists, and getting from one attraction to another is quite easy because of the subways, the taxis, and the tour shuttles....

B. Peer Review. Share your completed paragraph with a classmate. Have her/him respond to your first draft by writing the following on a separate sheet of paper:

Peer Response

1. Write two things that you found interesting about your classmate's paragraph.

2. Write two questions related to your classmate's paragraph.

3. Write two suggestions that you have for your classmate to incorporate into her/his next draft.

C. Expert Review. Share your draft with a native speaker who is an experienced writer—a peer at your school, a tutor, a writing-center instructor, or your writing professor. Ask for specific feedback about questions and concerns that you have about your paper. Your final draft will be evaluated on the areas listed in "Evaluation" below, so be sure to identify the areas and specific points on which you need the most help.

D. Revision. Use the feedback that you received from your reviewers to revise your paragraph. Write a final draft that incorporates improvements.

E. Evaluation. As you review and revise your paragraph, keep in mind that your writing will be evaluated on:

Ideas and Information—Is your paragraph detailed and specific enough to inform the reader? Do your have a focused topic supported by details?
Organization—Do you have a paragraph with logic, unity, and coherence?
Sentence Structure—Do you have complete sentences?
Word Use—Do you use content words appropriately? Are your transitions appropriate?
Punctuation Plus—Is your paragraph indented? Do you have capital letters at the beginning of sentences and full stops at the end?

2.5 Extend

Putting It All Together—In the "Engage" activity for this chapter, you looked at a classification scheme used by your library. Now, take a look at some other classification schemes. Choose two of the items below and—using your own resources, print resources in libraries and bookstores, and online resources—describe the classification schemes used for each.

1. How do biologists classify organisms?
2. How do chemists classify chemicals?
3. How do economists classify sectors of the economy?
4. How do department stores and catalogs organize their many products?
5. How do yellow pages categorize businesses?
6. How do Web portals categorize all of their information?

Beyond the Classroom—Most encyclopedias organize information alphabetically by topic. However, some like the *Encyclopaedia Britannica* attempt to create a classification system for all human knowledge. The *Britannica Propaedia* is an "Outline of Human Knowledge." Find the *Propaedia* in your college or local library and browse through it to see how its creator attempted to organize a huge amount of information.

Using Technology—Visit the U.S. Library of Congress electronically at <www.loc.gov>. The Library of Congress is the largest library in the world and it has many interesting and useful features online. Some of its Web pages will provide information on American history and culture, world culture, American government, and much more.

You can also use the online Library of Congress to search for books that you may want to look for in your own library or bookstore. Try the "Search Our Catalogs" link. You can search by author, title, or subject. See how many books the library has about your country.

Chapter 3—Narrative Writing

This chapter covers narration and its use in personal histories related to college applications and job applications.

3.1 Engage—The Mixer

The purpose of this activity is to help you quickly find out more about your classmates, share information about yourself, and learn to use speaking as a way of getting ideas to use in your writing.

Forming Groups: Use playing cards (enough numbered cards in all four suits to allow one card per student) to help divide the students for this activity. All the students should pick a card. They will use the number, the color, and the suit to group them for each part of the activity. When there are an odd number of students, a group of three can be used, or the professor can participate.

1. Find one other person with the same numbered card (A, 2, 3, 4 ...). Find a place where you can talk without interruption. Each member of your pair must speak for five minutes, one at a time. Introduce yourself. Give as many details as you can. Talk about your past, present, and future. Listeners should pay close attention, ask questions to help the speaker, but otherwise not interrupt. (Use about 10 minutes.)

2. Find another person with the same numbered card. Each member of your new pair must speak for two minutes, one at a time. Introduce yourself again. Focus on the most important details. Again, listeners should pay close attention, ask questions to help the speaker, but otherwise not interrupt. (Use about 5 minutes.)

3. Sit in a group with all of the students who have cards of the same suit (spades, hearts, clubs, or diamonds). The person with the highest numbered card is the recorder (the person who will write down your ideas). Make a list of the types of details you should include when introducing yourself. Think about what you would like to know about others. Keep in mind: past, present, and future. The list should have at least twenty-five or thirty details. (Use about 10 minutes.)

4. Work in your groups to choose the ten most important details to include whenever introducing yourself. The person with the lowest numbered card is the discussion leader (the person responsible for keeping the discussion going and focused on the task). Put a star next to the ten items on your list. (Use 5 minutes.)

5. Each individual student must now write one to two paragraphs (100 to 200 words). Introduce yourself; be sure to include the most important details identified by your group. Make the paragraphs as complete and well written as you can. (Use 15 minutes.)

6. Exchange your paragraphs with another student. Read your classmate's paragraphs. At the end of the paragraphs, write a sentence about something you found interesting. Write a question that you would like the writer to answer in the paragraphs.

3.2 Explore—Autobiographies and Biographies

When you introduced yourself, you were writing a short autobiography (a writing about your own life). Another type of writing is a biography (a writing about someone else's life).   There are many examples of autobiographies and biographies available in libraries, bookstores, and online.

Libraries

Reference Books—Libraries have encyclopedias, biographical dictionaries, and other reference books that contain several short biographies of important people, past and present. You can find biographies in the one-volume *Columbia Encyclopedia*, in all of the multi-volume encyclopedias, and in references such as *Current Biography*.
Books—Many libraries separate their autobiographies and biographies into their own section in the book stacks. These books are arranged alphabetically (A-Z) on the bookshelves by the last name of the subject of the book.
Periodicals—Journals that focus on culture and history, and popular magazines such as *American Heritage*, *Biography*, and *People* include many such articles.

Bookstores

Books and Periodicals—Bookstores have special sections full of biographies and also sell the popular magazines that explore people's lives.

Online

Use your favorite search engine to find autobiographies and biographies available on the Internet. Just type in <u>autobiography</u> OR <u>biography</u> on the search line and visit the sites highlighted.

Activity

1. Find examples of each type of autobiography/biography listed above. You will need to visit a library or bookstore and use the Internet. Use the information you gather to complete Table 3.1.

Table 3.1—Autobiographies and Biographies

Type	Name of source	Where did you find it?	Subject of the biography	Why is the person famous?
Reference book				
Book				
Magazine				
Website				

2. Choose one of the subjects of these biographies. Take 10 to 15 minutes to find out as much as possible about the person. If your source is a book, skim the book jacket, the table of contents, and the preface to get the main details. Write a one-paragraph summary of the person's life. Do NOT copy the information from the original source. Read it carefully. Write down notes about the main points. Put the original source away. Use your notes to write your summary. Share your summary with your teacher or classmates.

3.3 Explain—The Personal Narrative

Narrative writing tells a story. It typically uses chronological order (organization by time) to describe events that happen in a logical sequence from beginning to end. Narrative writing is useful in exploring experience, either one's own or someone else's.

Autobiographies and biographies are types of narrative writing that tell the stories of people's lives. They either tell the story of a person's life from birth to death or focus on a specific period in a person's life, usually a period of importance. Diaries and journals are types of autobiographical writing.

A **personal narrative** is a type of narrative writing that focuses on autobiographical details and usually relates them to a point or theme the writer is trying to develop. This type of writing allows writers to learn more about themselves and share what they have learned with others. Colleges, universities, and businesses often require a personal narrative as part of the application process.

In the following narrative, American writer Mark Twain (1835-1910; born Samuel Clemens) relates some of the events that led to his becoming a writer.

> There have been many turning-points in my life.... When I was twelve and a half years old, my father died. It was in the spring. The summer came, and brought with it an epidemic of measles. For a time a child died almost every day. The village was paralyzed with fright, distress, despair. Children that were not smitten with the disease were imprisoned in their homes to save them from the infection. In the homes there were no cheerful faces, there was no music, there was no singing but of solemn hymns, no voice but of prayer, no romping was allowed, no noise, no laughter, the family

moved spectrally about on tiptoe, in a ghostly hush. I was a prisoner. My soul was steeped in this awful dreariness—and in fear. At some time or other every day and every night a sudden shiver shook me to the marrow, and I said to myself, "There, I've got it! and I shall die." Life on these miserable terms was not worth living, and at last I made up my mind to get the disease and have it over, one way or the other. I escaped from the house and went to the house of a neighbor where a playmate of mine was very ill with the malady. When the chance offered I crept into his room and got into bed with him. I was discovered by his mother and sent back into captivity. But I had the disease; they could not take that from me. I came near to dying. The whole village was interested, and anxious, and sent for news of me every day; and not only once a day, but several times. Everybody believed I would die; but on the fourteenth day a change came for the worse and they were disappointed.

This was a turning-point of my life. (Link number one.) For when I got well my mother closed my school career and apprenticed me to a printer. She was tired of trying to keep me out of mischief, and the adventure of the measles decided her to put me into more masterful hands than hers.

I became a printer, and began to add one link after another to the chain which was to lead me into the literary profession. A long road, but I could not know that; and as I did not know what its goal was, or even that it had one, I was indifferent. Also contented.

From "The Turning-Point of My Life" in *What Is Man? and Other Essays of Mark Twain,* 1905

Related Structures

Narratives and Time

In narratives, the events of the story are related in time. Often the events progress in chronological order, from the first event through the last. At other times, the story jumps around in time. No matter how the events are related, it is important for the writer to indicate the time frame, so that the reader can follow along.

Indicating a time frame—A time frame is a period of time that begins at a specified time and ends at a later specified time. In English, we can indicate the time frame by using time phrases and time clauses. We can also indicate the time frame through verb tense.

Prepositions Used in Time Phrases

at—a specific time on the clock: at midnight (12:00 a.m.); at 2:30 in the morning (a.m.); at eight o'clock in the morning (8 a.m.); at noon (12:00 p.m.); at 3:36 in the afternoon (p.m.); at seven o'clock in the evening (7:00 p.m.); at 10:30 at night (p.m.).

at that—a specific focus: at that time; at that instant; at that moment; at that second; at that minute; at that hour; at that time of day; at that time of year.

around—an approximate time on the clock: around midnight; around 2:30 in the morning (a.m.); around noon (12:00 p.m.); around 3:30 in the afternoon (p.m.); around 10:30 at night (p.m.); around that time.

on—a day on the calendar: on Monday; on January 3; on July 4, 1776; on Labor Day; on Thanksgiving; on my birthday; on their anniversary; on the first of the month.

in—within the time frame indicated: in the morning; in the afternoon; in the evening; in the second week of March; in September; in the winter; in 1996; in the 1960s; in the 1800s; in the nineteenth century; in the first millennium; in the Jurassic Period.

before—within the time frame previous to the one indicated: before noon; before sunrise; before class; before Tuesday; before graduation; before February 6; before Christmas; before July; before spring; before 2001; before the 1950s; before the 1600s; before the twelfth century; before the Christian Era.

during—within the time frame indicated: during the class; during the night; during the weekend; during fall semester; during her vacation; during his stay in Egypt; during Clinton's second term; during the Ching Dynasty.

after—within the time frame subsequent to the one indicated: after midnight; after sunset; after lunch; after Saturday; after commencement; after August 8; after New Year's Day; after October; after summer; after 2000; after the 1860s; after the 1700s; after the eighth century; after the fall of Rome.

since—within the time frame that begins as indicated and that continues to the present: since 3:05 a.m.; since sunrise; since the start of the game; since Friday; since the beginning of the month; since 1978; since World War II; since the invention of the light bulb; since the arrival of Europeans in the Americas; since the third century B.C.; since the dawn of history.

by—within the time frame that ends as indicated: by 5:50 p.m.; by noon tomorrow; by Tuesday; by the fifteenth of the month; by February; by the end of the year; by 2020; by the 1770s.

between ___ and ___—within the time frame that begins and ends as indicated: between now and 10:00 p.m.; between January 1 and July 1; between 1939 and 1944.

from ___ to ___—within the time frame that begins and ends as indicated: from now to the end of class; from 2:10 to 3:15; from Memorial Day to Labor Day; from 1861 to 1864.

until—within the time frame before and up to the time indicated: until seven o'clock; until Sunday; until May; until the end of the year; until 1978; until the cows come home.

Adjectives Used with Time Words

every—a time frame that is repeated or habitual: every second; every minute, every hour, every morning; every day; every week; every month; every semester; every year.

every other—a time frame that repeats, skips, repeats, skips, and so on: every other day; every other Friday; every other week; every other month; every other semester; every other year.

this—within a time frame connected to the current time: this morning; this afternoon; today (= this day); tonight (= this night); this week; this month; this year; this decade; this century; this millennium.

last—within a time frame immediately before the current time frame: last night; yesterday (= last day); last Wednesday; last week; last month; last summer; last year.

next—within a time frame immediately after the current time frame: tomorrow (= next day); next Sunday; next week; next month; next fall; next year.

ago—during the time frame that occurred the indicated amount of time before now: twenty minutes ago; six hours ago; thirty days ago; 25 years ago; one million years ago.

Time Clauses

Remember, a clause is a group of words with its own subject and verb. A time clause is just a clause that sets the time frame. A time clause does not make a complete sentence. (It is a dependent clause.) Therefore, a time clause must accompany an independent clause. Some common clause markers that begin time clauses are:

when—when I was twelve and a half years old; when I got well ...
after—after I got well; after he learned the printing trade ...
before—before Twain was apprenticed; before he became a writer ...
since—since Twain established the American style; since the first Europeans arrived ...
until—until the printing press was invented; until the paperback made literature affordable ...

Verb Tenses

Language learners often hear about the 12 English verb tenses. In this book, we will look at the verb tenses a little differently.   We will look at time frames, time focus, and action.

Four Types of Time Frames

Past—The time frame has ended.
Present—The time frame has not ended.
Future—The time frame has not yet begun.
All—The time frame includes past, present, and future time frames.

Three Types of Time Focus

Before—The action occurs before the time index. (Perfect)
At that time—The action occurs at the time index. (Not Perfect)
After—The action occurs after the time index. (Not Perfect)

Three Types of Action

Habitual—The action repeats periodically or by habit. (Not Progressive)
Finished—The action has finished, or is permanent. (Not Progressive)
Unfinished—The action has not yet finished, or is temporary. (Progressive)

In order to determine the appropriate verb tense for a given situation, you must ask yourself these questions:

1. Is the time frame past, present, future, or all? See the descriptions above
2. Is the time focus before, at that time, or after? See the descriptions above.
3. Is the action habitual, finished (permanent), or unfinished (temporary). See the descriptions above.

After you have chosen, find the appropriate table (see Tables 2.2 through 2.5), column, and row. The verb tense or tenses that describe that combination of time frame, time focus, and action will be in the box.

Table 3.2—Past Time Frame

	Before	**At that time**	**After**
Habitual	past perfect	simple past	simple past
Finished (permanent)	past perfect	simple past	see Unfinished
Unfinished (temporary)	past perfect progressive	past progressive	past progressive

Table 3.3—Present Time Frame

	Before	**At that time**	**After**
Habitual	present perfect	simple present	simple present
Finished (permanent)	present perfect	simple present	see Unfinished
Unfinished (temporary)	present perfect progressive	present progressive	present progressive

Table 3.4—Future Time Frame

	Before	**At that time**	**After**
Habitual	future perfect	simple future	simple future
Finished (permanent)	future perfect	simple future	see Unfinished
Unfinished (temporary)	future perfect progressive	future progressive	future progressive

Table 3.5—All Time Frames

Simple present for all focuses and actions.

For a review of how to form simple, progressive, perfect, and perfect progressive in the past, present, and future time frames, see the "Extra" section at the end of the book.

3.4 Exercise / Evaluate

Exercise 1: Warm-up Writing

In a paragraph (10-12 sentences), tell the reader about a lesson that you once learned. Explain the lesson and tell the story of how you learned it. Your audience is your classmates and other peers. Your purpose for writing is to share your experience. Some examples of how to start such a paragraph are:

When I was twelve years old, I learned that adults do not know all the answers to life's important questions....

OR,

Traveling in a foreign country takes more than courage; it also takes physical stamina....

Exercise 2: Skill/Structure Practice

A. Organizing by Chronological Order—Below are several sentences about some famous travelers. First, put each group of sentences about a specific traveler into chronological order (order by time) from first to last. Use numbers 1 to 5. Number 1 is first in time, 2 is second, and so on to 5, the last. After you have finished all of the groups, decide which traveler should be placed first chronologically in a history book about travelers. Put an A in the blank next to that traveler's name. Organize the remainder of the travelers chronologically, using B, C, D, and E to designate the appropriate order.

Ibn Batuta _____

_____After visiting Mecca, Ibn Batuta explored the lands that are now known as Saudi Arabia, Iraq, and Iran.

_____Ibn Batuta became interested in exploration in 1325 while traveling through North Africa and Syria on a religious pilgrimage to Mecca.

_____After returning from China to Tangier in 1350, Ibn Batuta traveled first north across the Mediterranean Sea to Spain and then south across the Sahara Desert to Timbuktu in Mali.

_____For almost a decade in the 1330s and 1340s, Ibn Batuta lived in India and China.

_____Ibn Batuta, a famous explorer from what is now Morocco, was born in Tangier around 1300.

Christopher Columbus _____

_____After surviving a 1476 shipwreck off the coast of Portugal, Cristiforo Colombo of Genoa, Italy (known in English as Christopher Columbus) went to work in Lisbon as a mapmaker.

_____On October 12, 1492, Christopher Columbus and his expedition arrived at a small island in what is now the Bahamas Archipelago, a group of islands off the coast of Florida.

_____Christopher Columbus was not able to find someone to support his plan to establish a westward trade route to the Indies until 1492, when King Ferdinand and Queen Isabella of Spain agreed to provide him three ships and supplies.

_____Between 1493 and 1502, Christopher Columbus made three more voyages to the New World, establishing a Spanish colony on Hispaniola and exploring the coasts of South and Central America.

_____While living in Portugal, Christopher Columbus traveled on business to islands in the Atlantic Ocean and became convinced that he could sail west to reach the Indies, lands rich in spices.

Leif Eriksson

_____In 999, Leif Eriksson traveled to Norway, the homeland of his father, and after becoming a Christian, he set out to bring Christianity to the settlers in Greenland.

_____Leif Eriksson grew up in Greenland, a land that his father had discovered in 982 after being forced to leave Iceland because of a crime he had committed.

_____Sometime after 1000, Leif Eriksson sailed west beyond Greenland on a voyage that explored the far northeastern coast of the North American mainland, possibly Baffin Island, Labrador, Newfoundland, and Nova Scotia.

_____Leif Eriksson ended his life as the leader of the Norse settlement on Greenland.

_____Leif Eriksson was born sometime in the late 960s or early 970s in Iceland, where his father, the Norwegian voyager Eric Thorvaldson (Eric the Red) had settled.

Meriwether Lewis and William Clark _____

_____The Lewis and Clark Expedition left St. Louis in May of 1804 to travel up the Missouri River.

_____Meriwether Lewis and William Clark, along with the rest of their expedition, returned to St. Louis on September 23, 1806.

_____In 1805, with the help of the guide Sacajawea—a Native-American woman—the Lewis and Clark Expedition crossed the Rocky Mountains on horseback and then reached the Pacific Ocean by river.

_____Where the Mississippi and Missouri Rivers meet, Meriwether Lewis brought together his friend William Clark and dozens of military men and civilians late in 1803.

_____President Thomas Jefferson employed Meriwether Lewis to lead a Corps of Discovery to explore the Louisiana Territory, which had just been purchased from France in 1803.

Marco Polo _____

_____In 1295, Marco Polo and his father and uncle returned to Venice.

_____Marco Polo (1254-1324) joined his father, Niccolo, and his uncle, Maffeo—two traders from Venice—on a journey from Italy to China in 1271.

_____Marco Polo traveled to central China and India to conduct business for the khan.

_____While a prisoner of war from 1296 to 1298 in the conflict between the city-states of Venice and Genoa, Marco Polo first told stories of his travels to the east.

_____After arriving in the capital of the Mongol empire, Cambuluc (now Beijing), Marco Polo went to work for Kublai Khan.

B. Time Words—Fill each blank in the sentences below with an appropriate preposition or adjective. See the prepositions and adjectives listed in "Related Structures" above.

1. Many technological advances were made _____ the twentieth century, advances that helped make life longer and easier for those in the developed countries.

2. The first immigrants to North America probably used an ice bridge to cross from northeastern Asia to what is now Alaska more than 10,000 years _____.

3. The Great Depression had a serious effect on the economy of the United States, so _____ 1931 and 1940, only 530,000 immigrants came to this country, less than any decade since the 1830s.

4. Many people talked, danced, and walked around _____ the two hours that the band played, but when the food arrived, everyone sat down and ate quietly.

5. In the hot dog eating contest at the state fair, a man was able to eat fifteen hot dogs _____ five minutes.

6. Spanish explorers first introduced hot peppers to the Old World at the end of the 1400s, but _____ the end of the 1500s, they had already become an important part of cooking in India, China, and other parts of Asia.

7. Frank looks very tired this morning; because of the storm, he was not able to get much sleep _____ night.

8. No one had ever run a mile in less than four minutes _____ Roger Bannister did at Oxford University in 1954.

9. Comet Halley has a regular orbit that causes it to come close enough to the earth for easy viewing _____ seventy-six years.

10. The flight was scheduled to depart _____ 10:15 a.m. for Tokyo, but it was delayed because of mechanical problems.

11. Because of bad weather, the city was not able to hold the festival as scheduled, but the festival will be held on the same day _____ week.

12. Because he has to get up to go to work very early, Jerry goes to bed right _____ he finishes dinner.

13. Neil Armstrong became the first man to walk on the moon _____ July 21, 1969.

14. The witness was not sure exactly what time the robbery had occurred, but she thought it was _____ midnight.

15. The percentage of Americans who regularly use the Internet has grown _____ 1995 from less than 25 percent to greater than 50 percent.

C. Verb Tenses—Carefully consider the time words in the following sentences to determine the timeframe. Then fill in the blanks with the appropriate form of the verb given in parentheses ( ).

1. By the time Wilbur and Orville Wright became interested in flight, others like Otto Lilienthal (fly)_____ thousands of times in gliders.

2. While the Wright brothers (prepare)_____ for their first powered flight, Samuel P. Langley and his pilot Charles Manly attempted and failed to fly Langley's airplane, *Aerodrome*.

3. The Wright brothers (succeed) _____ in flying a heavier-than-air vehicle on December 17, 1903, near Kitty Hawk, North Carolina.

4. Ever since the Wright brother's first flight, people (try)_____ to extend flight to new records.

5. In 1927, Charles Lindbergh (arrive)_____ in Paris in his airplane, *The Spirit of St. Louis*, becoming the first person to fly alone non-stop across the Atlantic Ocean.

6. Amelia Earhart, the first woman to fly across the Atlantic Ocean alone, (attempt)_____ to fly around the world in 1937, but she and her copilot, Frederick Noonan, disappeared somewhere in the Pacific Ocean.

7. Chuck Yeager became the first person to fly faster than the speed of sound when, on October 14, 1947, he (pilot)_____ the Bell X-1 to a speed of approximately 800 miles per hour.

8. Although Neil Armstrong and eleven others walked on the moon between 1969 and 1972, no one (return)_____ to the moon since.

9. Today, several groups of engineers (work)_____ to build a safe and inexpensive vehicle to take people and cargo into space.

10. Perhaps someday everyone (be)_____ able to fly in space.

Exercise 3: Focused Writing Practice

Use the following notes to write a narrative of the life of Estevanico, a fascinating figure from the period of history when Europeans and Africans (as it turns out) were exploring the New World. Write grammatically correct complete sentences and put them together into well-organized paragraphs. You will need to add time words where necessary and change verbs into the appropriate tenses. You will also need to combine some ideas together into compound and complex sentences. (See the "Extra" chapter for more information about sentence types.) You should use almost all of the details provided in the notes. You may, however, decide to leave out a few facts if you find they are not important parts of the life of Estevanico. Remember, you are writing about Estevanico, so your main focus should be on him.

Notes for the events in the life Estevanico

- around 1503—born in Morocco
- Portugal has power in this area

- the Portuguese sell many of the people of this area into slavery
- 1520—Estevanico becomes servant of Andres Dorantes
- Dorantes is from Spain
- June 27, 1527—expedition of Panfilo de Narvaez leaves Spain
- the King of Spain wants Narvaez to conquer Florida and the lands near the Gulf of Mexico
- the expedition has 600 men
- Dorantes is part of the expedition
- Estevanico accompanies his master
- the expedition sails from Spain to Hispaniola
- the Dominican Republic and Haiti are on the island of Hispaniola
- the expedition sails to Cuba
- February 1528—the expedition leaves Cuba
- the expedition has 400 men
- the expedition travels around Florida to Tampa Bay
- May-June 1528—the expedition marches inland
- Narvaez wants to find gold
- many die of hunger and disease
- many killed by the native people
- they travel among the native Apalachee people
- they fight the Apalachee
- many die in battle, of hunger, or disease
- Narvaez decides to go to Mexico
- the Spanish build rafts
- the expedition has 250 men
- September 22, 1528—the Spanish sail west along the Gulf Coast
- November 1528—storm destroys rafts
- 80 survivors
- survivors land on Galveston Island, Texas
- winter 1528—survivors live with local native peoples
- spring 1529—15 alive
- native people take Spaniards and Estevanico inland in Texas
- 12 from the expedition escape
- Estevanico is in this group
- 1532—3 of 12 escapees are alive
- 1532—1 who has not escaped is alive
- 4 from expedition are captives of the native people
- the 4 are Estevanico, Dorantes, Alonso del Castillo, and Alvar Nunez Cabaza de Vaca
- Cabeza de Vaca is the author of *La Relacion* (*The Account*)
- *La Relacion* describes its author's adventures as part of the Narvaez expedition
- *La Relacion* is first published in 1555
- September 1534—4 escape from Native Americans
- 1534-1536—4 walk toward Mexico
- they see many things: American bison
- Estevanico learns many languages

- 4 serve as medicine men
- early 1536—4 find Spanish soldiers in northern Mexico
- summer 1536—they reach Mexico City
- Estevanico stays in Mexico City for 2 1/2 years
- Estevanico serves Antonio de Mendoza
- Antonio de Mendoza is the Viceroy of Mexico
- February 1539—Catholic monk Marcos de Niza forms an expedition
- the expedition searches for seven cities in the American Southwest
- the Spanish believe the seven cities are rich in gold
- Estevanico joins the expedition as guide
- March-April 1539—Estevanico guides the group north
- Estevanico knows the area/the people/their languages/experience as a medicine man
- Estevanico goes ahead to scout and send back information to the larger group
- May 1539—Estevanico encounters the Zuni people of northern New Mexico
- Estevanico was killed by one group of Zunis

Exercise 4: Personal Narrative Writing Assignment

This assignment gives you an opportunity to practice writing a personal narrative, a type of writing you may be asked to do in completing an application for college or university admission, or for a job. Narratives often use past tense verbs to give background information and to describe actions and experiences in past time frames; they use present tense verbs to give general information and to describe actions and experiences in the present time frame; they use future tense verbs to talk about plans, intentions, and hopes.

Writing a Personal Narrative. Choose one event from your life and use that event to explain why you are an excellent candidate for admission to college or university undergraduate study, acceptance into a university graduate program, or employment in a particular position. Your audience is the admissions department of the college or university or the hiring committee for a job. Your purpose is to convince your audience to accept you into the school or hire you for the job.

If you have trouble choosing an event to use, describe your first trip to the United States and explain how it shows qualities or characteristics (explain which characteristics) that are important for success in school or on the job.

Write three to five paragraphs. Make the paragraphs as complete and well written as you can.

For example,

> Universities want students who are academically strong, but they also want students who can contribute positively to the school and the community beyond. In 2000 when I arrived at the University of Tallinn from my hometown, I noticed that there were no computer labs available for students to use after 7:00 p.m. I decided that ....

Self-Review. After you have written your narrative, read it over to make sure that you have focused on the assignment and used time words and verb tenses appropriately.

Peer Review. Share your completed narrative writing with one of your classmates. Have her/him respond to your first draft by writing the following on a separate sheet of paper:

Peer Response

1. Write three things that you found interesting about your classmate's narrative.

2. Write three questions that you have now that you have read your classmate's narrative.

3. Write three suggestions that you have for your classmate to incorporate into her/his next draft.

Expert Review. Share your draft with a native speaker who is an experienced writer—a peer at your school, a tutor, a writing-center instructor, or your writing professor. Ask for specific feedback about questions and concerns that you have about your paper. Your final draft will be evaluated on the areas listed in the "Evaluation" section below, so be sure to identify the areas and specific points with which you need the most help.

Evaluation

Good writing has several important qualities from attention to minute details to a command of the big picture. To account for this, your writing will be evaluated on how well you address the requirements of the following five areas:

Ideas and Information—Is it detailed and specific enough to inform the reader? Do you have a focused topic supported by details?
Organization—Do you have paragraphs with logic, unity, and coherence?
Sentence Structure—Do you have complete sentences?
Word Use—Do you use content words appropriately? Are your transitions appropriate?
Punctuation Plus—Are your paragraphs indented? Do you have capital letters at the beginning of sentences and full stops at the end?

As you review and revise your writing, keep all five of these areas in mind.

3.5 Extend

Putting It All Together— In order to be admitted to a college or university, to earn a scholarship, or to land a job, you may have to participate in an interview. You will be more successful if you give some thought to the kinds of questions you might be asked and if you prepare your answers.

1. First, list five questions that you think you might be asked if:

a. you are interviewing for admission to a college or university;
b. you are interviewing to receive a scholarship;
c. you are interviewing for a job.

2. Choose one of the three types of interviews above and find one book in the library or at a bookstore related to that topic. Also, search the Internet for one source related to that topic. Compare the information from your research to your questions.

3. Work with a partner to practice being interviewed for whichever type of interview you chose.

Beyond the Classroom—Conduct research in your library, local bookstores, or online to find one of the following: (1) the top-ranked colleges and universities for various programs in the United States; (2) the best sources for scholarships for international students; OR (3) the jobs with the most growth expected in the next decade. Share your research with your classmates.

Use the information that you have gathered to select a university for further study, a helpful scholarship, or a job appropriate to your background and interests.

Chapter 4—Essay Development: Body Paragraphs

The next two chapters provide an introduction to the key components of good essays. The focus of this chapter is on the core of the essay, known as the body.

Engage—Just the Facts, Ma'am

This activity involves looking at evidence and using it to try to solve a mystery. The story is about an unusual event. See if you can explain what happened. First, read the story. Then, in groups of two to four, use the clues to suggest an explanation.

When Officer Edgar Allan Holmes and his partner Officer Humphrey Colombo were called to the Mosaic District of Metro City, they had a strange feeling. The Mosaic District had been settled by people from all over the world—Asia, Australia, Africa, Europe, North and South America. Because of its diverse populations, it was known for its exotic restaurants and entertainment; but it was also known for its exotic crimes. The two police officers were afraid that this would be such a case. The neighbors had called the police to report terrifying screams coming from the fourth-floor apartment of an old building in an Indonesian neighborhood. When they arrived at the apartment they found the door locked and forced it open. When Holmes entered the apartment, it was obvious that there had been a crime committed, but it was not clear what crime.

Holmes's initial reaction was that it had been a robbery. Several of the drawers in the room had been emptied onto the floor. The furniture had been turned over. A money box was open in the middle of the floor. But, there was something abnormal about the scene. The money box was still filled with money, more than ten thousand dollars. The mess in the room seemed to be random. There was no one in the apartment even though neighbors reported that no one had left through the door after the screams. And, as Colombo reported, all of the windows appeared to be locked. This would be a complex mystery, Holmes told himself.

Colombo went outside into the hall to gather more information from the neighbors. The first person he talked to was a young boy who lived across the hall. He was very excited. He offered many details but most of them were trivial; he talked about what he had been eating and watching on television. His knowledge of the event appeared superficial. Next, Colombo interviewed a more mature witness. His information was very good. He knew the precise time that the screams had begun and that no one had gone in or out of the apartment door since the screams. This older witness also reported that there had been other noises simultaneous to the screams. The noises sounded like a foreign language but he didn't know which one.

Inside, Holmes was still trying to figure out the scene. He found several strands of coarse red hair. He also found one window unlocked, but it did not seem feasible that any man had left the room through it. Outside the window there was a forty-foot fall to the alley below. The only other thing in sight was a tree in the park almost twenty feet across the street. In the park, there were also several trailers and trucks belonging to a small circus that was touring the districts of the city.

Holmes and Colombo left the scene of the crime with no solution to the mystery. Later that night, however, as he was watching a television news report about the circus, Holmes was given a clue. A solution to the mystery became evident when he investigated the park.

1. In your group, gather the evidence together. Put the evidence from the story in the appropriate place.

<u>Details</u>

Setting (the neighborhood)

Crime scene (the apartment)

Witness accounts (what people said)

What do you think Holmes's solution was? What do you think happened? Use the clues to suggest a logical explanation.

Sherlock Holmes, a famous fictional detective, always said, "When you have eliminated the impossible, whatever remains, however improbable, must be the truth."

On a separate sheet of paper, write the explanation that your group has come up with. Your teacher will collect all the answers. To find out what happened, find the short story by Edgar Allan Poe entitled "The Murders in Rue Morgue." Both this story and Poe's original, on which this story was based, share the same solution.

4.2 Explore—Types of Evidence

In order to prove a point, police investigators, writers, politicians, or others need evidence. Firmer evidence tends to hold up to criticism and changes that come with time. Softer evidence is easier to dispute and may change with time. Some types of evidence have some characteristics that are firm and other characteristics that are soft. In formal academic settings, firm evidence is usually preferred. However, in some situations, a soft touch is better. You will need to decide what combination of firm and soft evidence will be most convincing in a given situation. Table 4.1 compares different types of evidence categorized as firmer or softer.

Table 4.1—Evidence

Firmer Evidence	Softer Evidence

objective evidence:
    facts and statistics—information proven through repeated examination and analysis.
    observations—things that you or others have noted and that can be confirmed.
    records—historical information written down or stored.
    expert testimony—the judgment of someone who specializes in the topic.
	subjective evidence:
	    precedent—something should be because it was done before.
	    analogies—something is _____ because it is like something else that is _____.
	    experience—something is _____ because it happened to you or others.
	    opinion—judgment based on personal views and beliefs.

first-hand evidence—evidence that is direct from the source	**second-hand evidence**—indirect evidence reported by other than the original source
evidence that is unbiased—evidence provided by a source that has no interest or gain related to the evidence	**evidence that is biased**—evidence provided by a source that has interest or gain related to the evidence

Activity

Read each of the following statements. Decide whether the statement is firm evidence or soft evidence and explain why.

1. Thirty-eight percent of American households have two cars, according to the National Automobile Institute.

2. A friend of mine told me that she had read an article that said that average temperatures are two degrees hotter now than they were 30 years ago.

3. A woman will never be president because a woman has never been president.

4. According to my thermometer, it is 82 degrees Fahrenheit outside today.

5. Aerospace engineer James Houston has analyzed the photographs of UFOs and explains that they are distorted images of military aircraft.

6. Among Americans polled by the Gallup Agency, 48 percent said they believe that UFOs are real.

7. Divorce is a serious problem and it is getting more serious; almost everyone I know is divorced.

8. Emma Davis, a 100-year-old resident of New York City, said that this was the strangest weather she had ever seen.

9. Foreign students contribute approximately $12 billion annually to the U.S. economy, states a report by NAFSA, an organization of international educators.

10. The Jupiter Micron must not be a dangerous car, because 250,000 people bought it in 2003.

11. Men have greater endurance than women.

12. The 2000 census reports that the median age of Americans is 35.3 years old.

13. The country is like a crowded ship that is getting even more crowded; some day, it is going to tip over and sink.

14. The Descendants of Colonial Americans Organization claims that foreign students are taking away seats from American students.

15. The population of the United States is 282 million people.

16. Shipping logs show that almost 20,000 immigrants came into the United States through Philadelphia in 1853.

17. The weather in Washington, D.C., is too hot in the summer.

18. There are 583,000 foreign students in the United States.

19. Traditionally, courts have given custody of children to the mother after divorce.

20. UFOs must not exist; I have never seen one.

4.3 Explain—Essay Development

Some ideas, questions, or problems are too complex to be addressed with a single paragraph. They may require more development—two, three, four, or four thousand paragraphs. When this is the case, a writer can connect these paragraphs together into an essay, the next level of organized writing. **Essays** have the same important characteristics as paragraphs. They have a topic, a focus, supporting details, unity, and coherence. They also follow a similar structure. The main difference is that an essay has more development; it is larger and more detailed. An essay is like an expanded paragraph. (Table 4.2 shows how a paragraph is related to an essay.)

A balloon provides an analogy: An empty balloon is like a paragraph. It has a balloon shape, but it may be a little flat. It has color, and it may have a design, a picture, or words. As you blow the balloon up, it expands. This blowing up is like providing more development. The balloon becomes progressively larger, but it keeps the same basic shape. It also retains the same basic color, design, picture, or words. It is still a balloon; it's just a larger, more developed balloon.

Table 4.2—Comparison of a Paragraph to an Essay

Paragraph	Essay
Topic sentence—the main idea of a paragraph. It contains a topic and a focus that narrows the topic.	**Thesis statement**—the main idea of an essay. It contains a topic and a focus that narrows the topic, and follows the other characteristics of a good topic sentence. Its focus may be broader than the focus of a paragraph's topic sentence.
Clarifying sentence—an optional sentence that helps explain the topic sentence. It may have a definition, a description, or other details that help to make the main idea clear.	**Preview**—an optional sentence or two related to the thesis statement that clarifies it and gives the reader an idea of the subtopics to be developed.
Supporting sentences—sentences that develop the topic sentence. They provide the evidence that explores the topic, proves its assertion, answers its implied questions, or addresses its implied problem. A writer needs a few to several supporting sentences, enough to provide the necessary level of development.	**Body paragraphs**—supporting sentences that have been expanded into paragraphs. The supporting sentences of a paragraph become topic sentences in their own paragraphs in an essay. These subtopics of the thesis statement are then developed by adding more evidence.
Concluding sentence—a sentence that provides an end to the paragraph, either by referring back to the topic sentence or by referring outside the paragraph to other writing or to the world.	**Conclusion**—a paragraph that provides an end to the essay. It often contains a reflection of the thesis statement, a summary of the essay's main points, and a reconnection to the world beyond the essay.

The Body of an Essay

One meaning of the word *body* is the main part of something. The **body** of an essay is the main part of the essay. It is where the main idea of the essay is developed with various kinds of evidence. It is where the writer explores the idea, answers the question, or addresses the problem.

Outlining

Sometimes, to help plan and organize the body of an essay, a writer will use an outline. An outline is like a skeleton (bones) for the body. It is a framework of key ideas onto which the writer can add details in order to create a well-developed body. An outline clearly shows the relationship between ideas. For example:

A Basic Outline

Great Apes
A. Chimpanzees
B. Bonobos
C. Gorillas
D. Orangutans

Here is the same outline with added subtopics—the characteristics to be explored. Note that the outline helps build coherence by making clear that the same characteristics will be covered for each ape.

Great Apes

A. Chimpanzees
   1. Genus and species
   2. Home and Habitat
   3. Physical Characteristics
   4. Diet
   5. Behaviors

B. Bonobos
   1. Genus and species
   2. Home and Habitat
   3. Physical Characteristics
   4. Diet
   5. Behaviors

The same characteristics will be covered for gorillas and orangutans.

Here is the same outline with details added. The appropriate details would also be added for bonobos, gorillas, and orangutans.

Great Apes

A. Chimpanzees
    1. Genus and species
        Pan troglodytes
    2. Home and Habitat
        a. Central and West Africa
        b. forests and savannahs
    3. Physical Characteristics
        a. height—130 to 160 cm
        b. weight—40 to 70 kg
    4. Diet
        a. primarily plant eaters—fruit, nuts, tubers, and leaves
        b. insect eaters
        c. occasionally eat meat—small animals and monkeys
    5. Behaviors
        a. live in large groups, led by dominant male
        b. spend time in trees and on ground

4.4 Exercise / Evaluate

Exercise 1: Warm-up Writing

Use the following somewhat detailed outline to write a paragraph describing orangutans.

D. Orangutans
    1. Genus and species
        Pongo pygmaeus
    2. Home and Habitat
        a. Indonesia—islands of Borneo and Sumatra
        b. rainforests
    3. Physical Characteristics
        a. height—140 cm
        b. weight—82 kg
        c. known for reddish hair
        d. very long arms used for moving through trees
    4. Diet—fruit and seeds
    5. Behaviors
        a. adult males solitary; females and offspring grouped; juveniles sometimes grouped
        b. spend almost all of their time in trees; build a new nest every night

Exercise 2: Skill/Structure Practice

A. Add details to the topics below and then write a good thesis statement that incorporates both the topic and the details. Below each thesis statement, write an outline with characteristics to be explored for each. Use the outlines above as examples.

Meals of the Day

Seasons of the Year

Types of Music

Exercise 3: Focused Writing Practice

Writing the Essay Body. This exercise will give you practice writing the body section of an essay. Using the following outline, write three to five paragraphs to serve as the body of an essay about the education system in your country. Be sure to include as much detail as possible in each of the areas suggested in the outline. For each of the paragraphs that you write, be sure to use grammatically correct complete sentences and put them together to make well-organized paragraphs. Also, make sure that you keep in mind your focused topic, you provide logical support, you maintain unity, and you build coherence.

Outline: The Education System in _____

Thesis statement: _____ .

A. Preschool
    1. Purpose
    2. Ages of the children
    3. Characteristics of the education at this level
        a. Who teaches?
        b. What is taught?
        c. When and where is it taught?
        d. How is the material taught?
        e. How much does it cost families?

B. Elementary (or Primary) School
    1. Purpose
    2. Ages of the children
    3. Characteristics of the education at this level
        a. Who teaches?
        b. What is taught?
        c. When and where is it taught?
        d. How is the material taught?
        e. How much does it cost families?

C. Secondary School (high school)
    1. Purpose
    2. Ages of the children
    3. Characteristics of the education at this level
        a. Who teaches?
        b. What is taught?
        c. When and where is it taught?
        d. How is the material taught?
        e. How much does it cost families?

D. Higher Education
    1. Purpose
    2. Ages of the children/people
    3. Characteristics of the education at this level
        a. Who teaches?
        b. What is taught?
        c. When and where is it taught?
        d. How is the material taught?
        e. How much does it cost families?

4.5 Extend

Beyond the Classroom—Look for the short stories of Edgar Allan Poe, Sir Arthur Conan Doyle, and other mystery writers in your library, bookstore, or online. Read one or two. Mystery stories are fictional narratives that are quite unlike the type of nonfiction writing that is expected in academic settings. Mystery stories use suspense to keep the reader interested. Their writers keep the most important points hidden from the reader until the exciting climax. In most academic writing, the writer exposes the most important points in the very beginning of the writing and then goes on to develop them with details. For this reason, informative writing is sometimes called **exposition**.

Thinking Skills—Sometimes the evidence that you have available needs to be analyzed in order to use it. At these times, it is useful to know about logic and the various tools available in the area of logic. Deduction and induction are two such tools.

Deduction begins with something general that has been established to be true. If you begin with an established general truth, you can draw conclusions about particular cases by analyzing them against the established truth. Deduction uses rules and laws to help make specific judgments. For example:

All people born in the United States are American citizens.
Eun Ju Park was born in the United States.
Therefore, one would reason deductively that Eun Ju Park is an American citizen.

Induction begins with specific examples. After you analyze many examples, you may recognize a pattern or fact that is true about all of them. When you put your analysis all together and create a general truth about them, you are using induction. Induction uses observations and experience to arrive at new rules. For instance:

On an island in the Indian Ocean, a scientist observes one animal with a pouch. He then observes another, and another, and another, and another, and so on. After several examples, he reasons inductively that all animals on this island have pouches.

Using Technology—Many word processors have an outlining feature. Find out more about the outlining feature of your word processor. Play around with it to see how it works. Use one of the outlines in this chapter as your content and practice creating an outline. If your word processor has an automatic outline feature, try changing the style of the outline and pick the style you prefer.

Chapter 5—Essay Development: Introductions and Conclusions

This and the previous chapter provide an introduction to the key components of good essays. This chapter focuses on the beginning and end of a good essay, the introduction and conclusion.

5.1 Engage— "E Pluribus Unum" —From Many One

This activity gives you practice in attracting the attention of readers and capturing complex ideas in just a few words. Mottos, titles, and slogans are different types of word groups used to attract attention and convey a lot of information in a few words. Mottos, like the motto of the United States printed above, capture the essence of a country, organization, or other group. Titles, like the one for this book, provide an overview of what is contained in a book, article, or essay. Slogans such as "Got Milk?" are used by advertisers to sell a product or service.

Forming Groups: Students should organize alphabetically by surname (family name), A's first through Z's last. The first three in line will form one group, the next three another group, and so on. The last group may have two or four students as needed. The person in each group with the surname closest to A will be the group leader. This student is responsible for making sure the group stays on task. The person in each group with the surname closest to Z will be the reporter. This student will write down ideas. Everyone else in the group should help contribute.

1. In your groups, create a slogan to advertise your school, your English language program, or your major. Your goal is to attract more students, especially more international students. Your slogan should be a phrase or sentence that will both capture the characteristics of your school, program, or major and attract people to want to come. (Use 10 minutes.)

2. Now develop a 30-second to one-minute radio commercial to use with your slogan. The commercial can be a monologue (one voice) or a dialogue (two or more voices). It should advertise your school, program, or major in more detail than the slogan. It should include your slogan either at the beginning or the end. (Use 30 minutes.)

3. Bring together two or three groups. Have each group perform its commercial for the other group or groups. (Use 10 minutes.)

4. Have the leader of each group write the group's slogan on the blackboard (whiteboard or large piece of newsprint). Have all the students vote for the best slogan by writing their choices on a small piece of paper. The teacher will tally the votes. The top two vote getters will be sent to the college or program administrators for consideration. (Use 10 minutes.)

5.2 Explore—Famous Quotations

You may know the expression: "A picture paints a thousand words." It is true that a good picture can tell a complete story. A good title can capture the essence of a book, story, or article. Moreover, a good quotation can sum up a complex idea in a single sentence or two.

Here are a few quotations from famous people.

Confucius— "I hear and I forget. I see and I remember. I do and I understand."
Doyle, Sir Arthur Conan (as Sherlock Holmes)— "When you have eliminated the impossible, whatever remains, however improbable, must be the truth?"
Edison, Thomas— "Genius is one percent inspiration and ninety-nine percent perspiration."
Einstein, Albert — "If I have seen farther than others, it is because I was standing on the shoulders of giants."
Gandhi, Mohandas— "We must become the change we want to see."
Jefferson, Thomas— "One man with courage is a majority."
Kennedy, John F.— "My fellow Americans, ask not what your country can do for you; ask what you can do for your country."
King, Martin Luther— "Injustice anywhere is a threat to justice everywhere."
Lincoln, Abraham— "The ballot is stronger than the bullet."
Twain, Mark— "It is better to deserve honors and not have them than to have them and not deserve them."

A good quotation appropriate to your topic can be a good way to start a paragraph or essay. There are several reference books in libraries or bookstores and Internet Web sites that collect famous quotations. These quotations are categorized by the person who said them and by the subject that they refer to.

Activity

Find a book of famous quotations in a library or bookstore, or use your favorite search engine to search for "famous quotations." Find a quotation that refers to each of the subjects listed below. Copy the quotation and the name of the person who said/wrote it. Explain in a few words what the quotation means.

anger—

crime—

education—

freedom—

guns—

happiness—

marriage—

men and/or women—

terrorism—

wisdom—

5.3 Explain—Introductions and Conclusions

In the previous chapter, you looked at the body of the essay. It is true that the body is the main part of the essay. It is also true that the simplest and most direct type of essay would be a thesis statement followed by a body that supports it. However, beginning with the thesis statement (the main idea) and then moving immediately to the body (where the main idea is developed) is considered too direct and abrupt for most formal writing contexts.

The Introduction

In most contexts, a writer should prepare a reader for the idea to be developed. The writer should attract the reader's attention and spark the reader's interest in the thesis. He or she should orient the reader to the thesis by providing background information or by connecting the thesis to the reader's experience. The writer should create a transition from the millions of ideas in the world to the specific ideas in this essay. This is the purpose of the first paragraph of an essay, the **introduction**.

The introduction is a special type of paragraph that helps prepare a reader for the idea to be developed in an essay. It has a different structure than a standard paragraph or the body paragraphs of an essay.

The Structure of an Introduction

An introduction includes the following elements.

Invitation—The invitation is a sentence that attracts attention and sparks interest in the thesis. A quotation is one type of invitation. It is appropriate for essays for some audiences and some contexts. Here is a list of several types of invitations. You can get a sense of which types are appropriate and effective for certain audiences and contexts by reading examples of good writing.

Types of Invitations

A quotation
A question
A surprising comment

A brief definition
A general statement of fact
An explanation of the topic's importance
An explanation of the topic's timeliness
An appeal to common experience
An anecdote—a brief story related to the topic

Orientation—The orientation includes a few to several sentences that provide background information on the thesis or connects the thesis to the reader's experience. The orientation also helps the reader make the transition from the general world to the specific idea of the thesis.

Proposition—The proposition tells the reader what the essay is going to be about. It must have a thesis statement and may have a preview. (In other words, the preview is optional.)

- **Thesis Statement**—The thesis statement establishes the idea that unifies the essay, the idea that the writer will explore and develop with evidence.
- **Preview**—The preview is a sentence or two that may (but does not have to) follow the thesis statement. It allows the writer to clarify a complicated thesis and to provide the reader a look at the subtopics that will be covered in the body.

The Conclusion

Just as beginning with the thesis statement and then moving immediately to the body is considered too direct and abrupt, stopping immediately after the body is also considered too direct and abrupt. In most contexts, a writer should reflect on the ideas developed in the body, remind the reader what has been learned, and release the reader to leave the specific ideas of the essay and return to the general world. This is the purpose of the last paragraph of the essay, the **conclusion**.

The conclusion is a special type of paragraph that helps the reader look back on the essay and then move on, somehow changed—having been informed, entertained, inspired, or persuaded. The structure of the conclusion is a mirror image of the structure of the introduction. It progresses from specific back to general.

The Structure of a Conclusion

A conclusion includes the following elements.

Transition—The conclusion sometimes (but not always) includes a transition word, phrase, or sentence to let the reader know that the body has been completed and the essay is soon to end.

Reflection—The introduction looks ahead to the development of the main idea of the essay in the body paragraphs. It has the thesis, a proposal (a promise) of what the writer will explain to the reader. It also has a preview of the subtopics to be included. The reflection often contains a review, a summary of the ideas developed in the body. It also often includes a restatement of the thesis in different words. This restatement reflects back on the ideas already explained in the body and therefore has the weight of something that has been established.

Resolution—The resolution includes a sentence or two that reorients readers to the world, a final thought that leaves readers with a feeling that they have been informed, entertained, inspired, or persuaded. It completes the essay.

Related Structures

Direct Quotes

Occasionally as a part of your essay—in the invitation or resolution, or to make a point in your body—you will want to use a quote. In the "Explore" section of this chapter, we looked at some quotations of famous people. When you quote someone in your paper, it is important that you take certain steps.

1. Use exact words—Direct quotes should use the exact words of the speaker or writer quoted: Injustice anywhere is a threat to justice everywhere.

2. Include quotation marks—The exact words should be indicated with quotation marks before and after the quoted words: "_____." For example: "Injustice anywhere is a threat to justice everywhere." If the source that you quote includes a quote from another source, the quote within your quote should be indicated with single quotation marks: '_____.' "I have a dream that one day this nation will rise up and live out the true meaning of its creed: 'We hold these truths to be self-evident: that all men are created equal.' "

3. Provide attribution—You must tell the reader who said or wrote the words quoted and provide information about where you found the words. "I have a dream that one day this nation will rise up and live out the true meaning of its creed: 'We hold these truths to be self-evident: that all men are created equal.' "—Martin Luther King, Jr., in a speech delivered in Washington, D.C., on August 28, 1963.

4. Establish the authority of the quote—Unless everyone knows the person who said the words, you should give some information about the speaker or writer. For example: Martin Luther King, Jr., was an American civil rights leader.

5. Present correctly—You must present the quote using correct grammar and punctuation in a way that fits smoothly into your paragraph or essay. For example: As American civil rights leader Martin Luther King, Jr., said in a speech delivered in Washington, D.C., on August 28, 1963, "I have a dream that one day this nation will rise up and live out the true meaning of its creed: 'We hold these truths to be self-evident: that all men are created equal.' "

Reported Speech

You can also include the ideas of others in your writing without quoting the exact words. In doing this, it is still important that you use the ideas of attribution, authority, and presentation, as explained above. But, instead of quoting the exact words, you change them, either slightly or quite a bit.

One way to do this is through reported speech. Reported speech involves slightly changing a quote so that you still capture the ideas of the original quote and you use many of the same words in the same basic sentence structure. A clause marker like *that* is used to introduce the slightly changed quote. An example would be: American civil rights leader Martin Luther King, Jr., said in a speech delivered in Washington, D.C., on August 28, 1963, that he had a dream that America would one day live up to its ideal of equality for all.

Paraphrasing and Summarizing

Another approach is through paraphrasing. When you refer to the ideas of others in your own words, it is called **paraphrasing**. Again, paraphrasing involves attribution, authority, and presentation. However, it does not quote the original words exactly.

A paraphrase may be as long as or longer than the original quote. When you have a long original to paraphrase, it is usually wise to focus on the key points in order to write a paraphrase that is shorter than the original. Paraphrasing and significantly shortening an original text is called **summarizing**.

To paraphrase or summarize effectively, you can use a few strategies, separately or in combination. Remember, preserve the key ideas, but

Change the words. Use synonyms (words with similar meanings) or antonyms (words with the opposite meaning) with *not*. For example: dream = hope for the future

Change the word forms. Transform nouns into verbs, verbs into nouns, adjectives into nouns, nouns into adjectives, and so on. For instance: a dream = dream (verb)

Change the sentence structure. Move things around in the sentences or create sentences with different structures. For example: The idea of equality will finally come true.

For example: American civil rights leader Martin Luther King, Jr., said in a speech delivered in Washington D.C., on August 28, 1963, that his hope for the future was that equality would finally come true.

Other Important Points

Verbs. There are several verbs that you can use to introduce quotes, reported speech, and paraphrases. Here, in context, are some of the verbs most commonly used:

Confucius asked, "...
Doyle claimed that ...
Edison commented that ...
Einstein declared, "...
Gandhi found that ...
Jefferson maintained, "...
Kennedy noted that ...
King observed, "
Lincoln pointed out that ...
Twain said, "...
Washington stated, "...
Yeats wrote, "...

Verb tense and other time words. Direct quotes capture the subject, the verb tense, and the time words exactly as they occurred in the original. The time that quotes were said is expressed in the phrase that introduces the quote. In reported speech, the subject, the verb tense, and the time words must change to fit the introductory phrase.

Now he says, "I am the one."   Now he says that he is the one.
Yesterday he said, "I am the one."   Yesterday he said that he was the one.

She says, "They will not arrive before tomorrow."
She says that they will not arrive before tomorrow.

She said, "They will not arrive before tomorrow."
She said that they would not arrive before the next day.

Frank and John claim, "Our sister won the lottery yesterday."
Frank and John claim that their sister won the lottery yesterday.

Frank and John claimed, "Our sister won the lottery yesterday."
Frank and John claimed that their sister had won the lottery the day before.

5.4 Exercise / Evaluate

Exercise 1: Warm-up Writing

Using your outline from Chapter 4, write an introductory paragraph and a conclusion paragraph for an essay about one of the following: Great Apes; Meals of the Day; Seasons of the Year; or Types of Music. Be sure to include all of the necessary elements.

Topic _____

I. Introduction

A. Invitation—

B. Orientation—

C. Proposition:
     Thesis statement—

     Preview—

III. Conclusion

A. Transition—

B. Reflection:
     Review—

     Restatement—

C. Resolution—

Exercise 2: Related Structure/Skill Practice

Use the name of the famous person plus a verb to introduce his famous quote in reported speech form.

For example:

Will Rogers — "We can't all be heroes because someone has to sit on the curb and clap as they go by."
Will Rogers observed that not all people could be heroes because someone had to sit on the curb and clap as they went by.

1. Confucius— "I hear and I forget. I see and I remember. I do and I understand."
2. Sir Arthur Conan Doyle — "When you have eliminated the impossible, whatever remains, however improbable, must be the truth."
3. Thomas Edison — "Genius is one percent inspiration and ninety-nine percent perspiration."
4. Albert Einstein — "If I have seen farther than others, it is because I was standing on the shoulders of giants."
5. Mohandas Gandhi — "We must become the change we want to see."

6. Thomas Jefferson — "One man with courage is a majority."
John F. Kennedy — "My fellow Americans, ask not what your country can do for you; ask what you can do for your country."
7. Martin Luther King — "Injustice anywhere is a threat to justice everywhere."
8. Abraham Lincoln— "The ballot is stronger than the bullet."
9. Mark Twain — "It is better to deserve honors and not have them than to have them and not deserve them."

Exercise 3: Focused Writing Practice

This exercise will give you practice writing the introduction and conclusion paragraphs of an essay. For background, use the body paragraphs that you wrote for Chapter 4 about the education system in your home country and add an introduction and a conclusion for that essay. Be sure to include information for each element.

The Education System in _____

I. Introduction

A. Invitation—

B. Orientation—

C. Proposition:
     Thesis statement—

     Preview—

II. Body

A. Preschool
B. Elementary (or Primary) School
C. Secondary School (high school)
D. Higher Education

III. Conclusion

A. Transition—

B. Reflection:
     Review—

     Restatement—

C. Resolution—

Exercise 4: Essay Writing Assignment

Writing the Essay. Put the body that you wrote for Chapter 4 together with the introduction and conclusion that you wrote for this chapter to make a unified and coherent essay.

Self-Review. After you have written your essay, read it over to make sure that you have included all of the elements of introductions, bodies, and conclusions.

Peer Review. Share your completed essay with one of your classmates. Have her/him respond to your first draft by writing the following on a separate sheet of paper:

Peer Response

1. Write three things that you found interesting about your classmate's essay.

2. Write three questions that you have now that you have read your classmate's essay.

3. Write three suggestions that you have for your classmate to incorporate into her/his next draft.

Expert Review. Share your draft with a native speaker who is an experienced writer—a peer at your school, a tutor, a writing center instructor, or your writing professor. Ask for specific feedback about questions and concerns that you have about your paper. Your final draft will be evaluated on the areas listed in the "Evaluation" section below, so be sure to identify the areas and specific points with which you need the most help.

Evaluation

Good writing has several important qualities, from attention to minute details to a command of the big picture. To account for this, your writing will be evaluated on how well you address the requirements of the following five areas:

Ideas and Information—Is it detailed and specific enough to inform the reader? Do your have a focused topic supported by details?
Organization—Do you have paragraphs with logic, unity, and coherence?
Sentence Structure—Do you have complete sentences?
Word Use—Do you use content words appropriately? Are your transitions appropriate?
Punctuation Plus—Are your paragraphs indented? Do you have capital letters at the beginning of sentences and full stops at the end?

As you review and revise your writing, keep all five of these areas in mind.

5.5 Extend

Beyond the Classroom—Advertising in print and on electronic media uses slogans to help sell products. Good advertising captures the qualities of a product and presents that product effectively to its chosen market. Bad advertising fails to capture the product's qualities and target its market. False advertising uses deceptive practices to try to trick consumers into buying products. Some examples of deceptive practices include:

Bait and switch—Advertising one product at a low price and then convincing the consumer to buy a higher-priced item instead.
False guarantees—Advertising guarantees on the performance or quality of the item, guarantees that do not exist or do not cover the cost of the product.
False sales or discounts—Portraying the price of an item as a sale or discount when it is not.
Unsupported claims—Making claims about the product's performance or quality that are not supported by evidence.

Find five advertisements in newspapers or magazines, or on television or the Internet. Look at the slogans used, the other words, and the images. Evaluate each ad on its ability to capture the qualities of the product, to target its market, and to meet standards of honesty.

Using Technology—A number of Web sites collect slogans and advertisements as examples of good and bad advertising campaigns. Type "advertising campaigns," "famous slogans," "advertising slogans," or similar keywords into your favorite search engine. Choose three slogans or advertisements and try to explain their effectiveness and appeal to your classmates.

Chapter 6—Process Writing

This chapter introduces the process essay and its uses in everyday, social science, and science contexts.

6.1 Engage—Studying in a Foreign Country

This activity is designed to use your knowledge and experience to help you learn and write about processes—instructions written to explain how to do something step by step.

Forming Groups: Students should organize in a line with the person born earliest in the year (closest to January 1) first and then chronologically by birthday through the year to the person born latest in the year (closest to December 31). Remember from Chapter 3 that chronology (by time) is one form of organization. The first three in line will form one group, the next three another group, and so on. The last group may have two or four students as needed. The person in each group with the earliest birthday will be the group leader. This student is responsible for making sure the group stays on task. The person in each group with the latest birthday will be the reporter. This student will write down ideas and report them to the whole class. Everyone else in the group should help contribute.

1. Each group needs to answer the question: "If students want to leave home to study in a foreign country, what are the steps, in order, that they must take to reach their goal?" Brainstorm steps required to study in a foreign country. (See "Before Writing—Special Tools" below for an explanation of brainstorming.) After you have listed many steps, reorganize them in sequence (in order by first, second, third, and so on). (Use about 15 minutes.)

2. Meet with a neighboring group or two. Find out if they have included steps that you have overlooked. Add any steps that you have missed in the appropriate order to your list. Combine steps where appropriate. Share your steps with them. (Use about 10 minutes.)

3. Have your group reporter mark off a portion of the blackboard (or whiteboard, or use a large piece of newsprint) and write your list of steps in order. (Use about 10 minutes.)

4. As a whole class, compare the lists of steps. Decide together which seven to ten steps are most important to success in reaching the goal of studying in a foreign country. (Use 10 minutes.)

5. Each individual student must now write one to two paragraphs (100-200 words). Explain that if students want to study in a foreign country, they must take these important steps in this order. Make the paragraphs as complete and well written as you can. (Use 15 minutes.)

6.2 Explore—Types of Process Writing

When you explain something step by step, either through speaking or writing, you are describing a process. Demonstrations, directions, and instructions involve describing processes. Because people like to do things, and they like to learn how to do things that they do not already know how to do, describing processes is a very valuable way for experts to share their knowledge with others.

Common Process Writing

Think about your day-to-day life. What are some common forms of process writing that you use on a regular basis? Think about home, school, and public contexts. Using Table 6.1 or a separate sheet of paper, list five processes that you can think of and give brief explanations of why they are written down for others.

Table 6.1—Process Writing

Type	Why written
1.	
2.	
3.	
4.	
5.	

Libraries, Bookstores, and Online

In addition to the common types of process writing that we encounter regularly, there are also many books written about processes. Books about processes often have titles that include: (1) **how to**..., such as *How to Read a Book*; (2) **guide or tutorial**, such as *The Complete Idiot's Guide* series; (3) **manual**, such as *The Gregg Reference Manual*; (4) **handbook**, such as *MLA Handbook for Writers of Research Papers*; or (5) **-ing words**, such as the _____ -ing for Dummies series.

Activity

1. Visit your college library or public library, a bookstore, or use your favorite Internet search engine to find online bookstores. Use the keywords above to help you in your search. Find five examples of books about processes, one for each keyword. Write the author's name and complete title.

how to—

guide—

manual—

handbook—

-ing word—

6.3 Explain—The Writing Process

"The longest journey begins with a single step."—Chinese Proverb

Writing is a difficult activity. It requires a lot of mental energy and a certain amount of physical energy on the part of the writer. It also requires a lot of time. At the beginning, seeing the end of a writing project is difficult for writers. Faced with the barriers to writing, writers often become blocked or frozen. They see themselves at the bottom of a mountain with a feeling that climbing it is impossible.

The writing process gives writers a way of overcoming these barriers. It breaks writing down into a series of small steps. Writers do not have to see all the way to the end of the project. They just have to focus on the task immediately ahead. By working on the parts, step by step, writers can arrive at the end with less mental and physical energy. They climb the mountain one step at a time.

There are three main parts of the writing process: what the writer does before writing, during writing, and after writing. Just remember: before, during, and after. What follows is a detailed explanation of the steps in the writing process. For a quick overview, see the "Extra" section at the end of the book.

The Writing Process

I. Before Writing

A. Getting Ideas

If you are like many writers, you feel that getting ideas is one of the hardest steps in the writing process. "I can't think of anything to write about," is a common response to a writing assignment. However, the truth is that there are ideas everywhere. We are surrounded by ideas. They constantly knock on our doors, wanting to be let in. Let them in. Here are some tools to make letting them in easier.

1. From Yourself

a. Knowledge
  - Analyzing—Break a subject into its parts. Think about the relationship of the parts to the whole.

- Brainstorming—Write down everything that comes into your mind about a topic. Everything. Do not judge the ideas as good, bad, serious, or silly. Just write them all down.
- Combining—Combine parts of a subject into a whole. Think about the relationship of the whole to the parts.
- Free Writing—Just write sentences without stopping for 10 to 15 minutes. Put down whatever comes into your head, in general or about a specific topic. Focus on ideas, not grammar and mechanics.
- Listing—Make lists of characteristics related to your topic. Group similar things together.
- Questioning—Use the wh- questions (who, what, when, where, why, how) to explore a subject.

b. Experience
- Describing—Carry a pocket-sized notebook. When you find something interesting, write it down in a little notebook that you always carry with you. This will help you remember what you have found.
- Journaling—Write a diary or journal. At the end of each day or week, look back and write down what has happened. Pick something interesting that came up and explain it.
- Observing—Open up. Whenever you read, write, draw, listen to the radio or music, watch television or movies, or whatever you do, keep your senses open for interesting ideas.

2. From Others

a. Primary Research—If you gather information from others through your own efforts, it is primary research.
- Corresponding—Letter writing used to be a good way of generating information. Now e-mail makes this even easier. E-mail provides a quick and convenient means of discussing, interviewing, and surveying.
- Discussing—Talk with family, friends, and acquaintances about their experiences and yours.
- Interviewing—People with expertise in a subject area are a good source of information. Ask the right questions and gather convincing evidence from these experts.
- Surveying—When you ask questions in a systematic way to get answers that are quantifiable and comparable, you are conducting a survey.
- Experimenting—By conducting experiments using formal methods, you can uncover new ideas, information, and data.

b. Secondary Research—If you seek out and use primary research created through the efforts of others, it is secondary research. Secondary research involves finding information by listening, reading, or watching. Sometimes you may have the start of an idea, but you require information to stimulate more ideas. A little secondary research can help.

B. Grouping Ideas

After you have ideas, you need to look for relationships among the various ideas. Can the ideas be organized according to time or space? Are some ideas similar, some different? Are some ideas positive and others negative? Do some ideas cause others? Do the ideas fit into different categories? Some common organizing schemes are listed below. Each can be used alone or combined with others.

Chronology—You used this in your narrative writing in Chapter 3. This is organization by time; we use it to relate events as they occurred from beginning to end.
Sequence—This is similar to chronological order, but in this case it is organization by the order that steps happen in a process; you can use it to relate which step is first, second, and so on.
Classification—Ideas with a similar characteristic can be put together into categories (or classes) that name the similar characteristic.
General to specific or specific to general—You can present the whole or general idea and then describe the parts or details that make up the whole. Or, you can present the details first and build up to the whole.
Most to least or least to most—When things or ideas within a category have different values, they can be put in order from most (biggest, most important, most expensive) to least (smallest, least important, least expensive). Or, you can reverse the order, organizing from the least to the most.

To help clearly show the relationships between ideas, you can use visual aids in grouping. Some examples of visual aids are included in Figure 6.1.

Figure 6.1—Visual Aids for Grouping Ideas

Timelines

1936   1953   1972   2001 ⟶

Tables

Charts, Diagrams, or Maps

Webs or Flowcharts

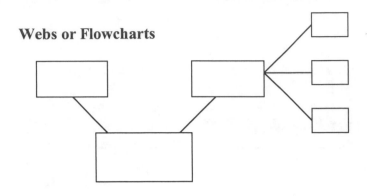

II. During Writing

A. Planning

1. Establishing the Writing Context—After you have gotten you ideas and grouped them, you need to prepare for the actual writing. One good way to do this is to answer the wh- questions (who, what, when, where, why, how, and which) with the writing in mind. Answering these questions helps you think ahead to what needs to be done. (See below for more information.)

Whom do you want to read your writing? (Don't just write for your teacher.)
What are you writing? (A letter; a paragraph; an essay; an article; a story; a memo; a report; others.) What rhetorical form will you use?
When will you write? When is the writing due? In what time frame is the subject set?
Where will you write? (In class; at home.) Do you have a good place, without distractions, to write? In what location is the subject set?
Why are you writing?
How will you write? (Pencil and paper; computer.) What approach will you use? (Writing process or other.)
Which sources will you use? (Yourself or others.) Which resources would be of help as you write?

Planning Table

Table 6.2—The Writing Context

Whom? (Audience)	
What? (Form)	
When? (Setting)	
Where? (Setting)	
Why? (Purpose)	
How? (Process)	
Which? (Source)	

Audiences for Writing (Whom?)

General readers—This includes everybody.
Specific groups—This includes only those people who have certain characteristics.
Experts—These are people who have a lot of knowledge of and experience with specific
topics.
Your peers—These are people with whom you have many characteristics in common.
One person—This is one specific person.
Yourself—This is you.

Purposes for Writing

To Share or Express
To Inform or Explain
To Prove or Persuade

Expressing Ideas (How?)

When you are writing, you are expressing ideas. For now, you are going to focus on expressing your own ideas. Later, you will explore how you can use the ideas of others in your writing.

In order to choose the best way to express your ideas, it is important that you keep in mind the wh- questions that you answered in planning. Depending especially on **whom** you are writing for, **what** you are writing, and **why** you are writing, you will have to choose the most appropriate **style**. Style is not just about how you dress; it is also about how you write. In choosing your style, you will have to think about several things. Three of these things are:

Register—Register has to do with the level of formality of your writing. Is it formal or informal? How important are grammar, spelling, punctuation, and other mechanics of writing? Register also includes an awareness of the common language of your audience. Can you use slang or other popular constructions? Written communication, especially in academic contexts, tends to be formal. Grammar, spelling, punctuation, and other mechanics follow standard guidelines. Vocabulary usually avoids slang and other popular constructions.

Level of sophistication—Sophistication concerns the level of thought expressed. Colleges, universities, and businesses expect thinking that goes beneath the surface, that explores a topic in depth, and that probes beyond the obvious. They expect writers to analyze ideas in detail, to use a critical eye, and to employ sound reasoning.

Tone—Tone is the character of the writing. Is it serious? Funny? Sincere? Sarcastic? Open? Mysterious?

Resources for Writers (Which?)

In addition to the necessary writing tools (pencils or pens and paper, or computers and printers), you should have other resources available to you when writing.

Learner's dictionary—Several publishers offer dictionaries designed specifically for ESL students. These dictionaries offer easy-to-understand definitions and example sentences.

Thesaurus—Thesauruses give synonyms (same meaning) and antonyms (opposite meaning) for words. They help writers use variety in their vocabulary. Several publishers offer thesauruses, but you may find that a dictionary-style (words listed in alphabetical order) thesaurus is easier to use than a Roget's thesaurus.

Writer's handbook—Several publishers have detailed handbooks that explain the process and mechanics of writing. Your college bookstore may have the handbook used in the college's writing courses.

Concise encyclopedia—Concise (or short) encyclopedias are one-volume encyclopedias with a lot of useful information. Some examples are *The Britannica Concise Encyclopedia*, *The Concise Columbia Encyclopedia*, *The New York Public Library Desk Reference*, and *The Random House Encyclopedia*.

Almanac—Almanacs are published every year to chronicle the events of the previous year, but they also contain a lot of general facts and figures. Many companies publish them.

Online resources—Many of these writing tools are now available on the Internet. On the search line of your favorite search engine, type in the name of the item you want to find and follow the links.

2. <u>Formulating a Main Idea</u>—The main idea should contain a topic and a focus. The formal main idea is the thesis statement. A thesis statement follows the same guidelines as the topic sentence for a paragraph.

a. A thesis statement includes a topic (general idea, question, or problem to be explored) and the focus that limits the topic. Focusing tools (specific aspects) include:

- time
- place
- number or sequence
- category or characteristic
- similarity or difference
- quality (good, bad, or other)
- cause or effect
- problem or solution

b. Strong thesis statements place the topic in the subject position of the sentence. For this reason, strong topic sentences do not begin with "There is/are" or "It is/They are." For example, "Competitive badminton is very different from the backyard version." is better than "There are a lot of differences between competitive badminton and the backyard version."

c. Strong thesis statements are statements (never questions) that require further development. They are not obvious statements that can be completely explained in a single sentence. In other words, "Benjamin's shirt is blue" is not a good topic sentence because it does not require any development. "Benjamin dresses in a way that reflects his personality." is better because it needs to be explained.

3. Developing Support—Use ideas from yourself and others to provide details that elaborate on the main idea. Supporting details come from the types of evidence discussed in Chapter 4.

a. Objective Evidence
  • Facts and statistics
  • Observations
  • Records
  • Expert testimony

b. Subjective Evidence
  • Precedents
  • Analogies
  • Experiences
  • Opinions

4. Organizing

a. Outlining—You will learn more about this and other organizing techniques in later chapters.

B. Writing

Writing involves writing. That seems obvious. But, the fact is that words, sentences, paragraphs, essays, and books do not write themselves. People—writers like you—have to write them. And, writers have to expend a significant amount of energy in order to write. So, whether you plan to use pencil and paper, old-fashioned typewriter, or computer, you have to prepare yourself to give the necessary effort. Just remember though, if you have a meaningful purpose for writing, an audience that you want to have read the writing, and a topic that interests you, AND if you use the writing process, you will find the journey easier and perhaps even more enjoyable.

As you write, you may want to try some of these **writing techniques** to help you along your way.

1. One Step after Another—The longest journey begins with a single step, and then continues one step after another. One writing technique is to begin writing and continue writing, one word after another, until you have finished.   You don't worry about writing fast or slow, carefully or carelessly. You just keep writing. This type of writing may not give a perfect draft, but it allows you to get your ideas down, and it puts words, sentences, and paragraphs on paper. After the words are on paper, it may be easier for you to understand what you have, what you want, and how you can make changes to improve the writing. This technique is especially useful if you have very little time or if you find yourself blocked.

2. Body First—A young man may find dancing with his girlfriend painfully difficult because his mind is trying to think how to approach, introduce himself, where to put the left hand and the right, how to stand, when each foot should move. The solution is often to let the body go first, free of the mind's inhibitions. Writers are sometimes inhibited because they are trying to decide how to start. One solution is to write the body first. Jump right into the main part of the essay. Often after the body has been developed, the introduction and conclusion come naturally.

3. Outside In—House builders usually build the foundation first, then put up the main supports, and then put on the roof. After they have covered the outside, they go inside to complete the interior. Writers can start with their thesis statement (the foundation), add the topic sentences for each paragraph (the main supports), and then write the concluding sentence (the roof). With the framework in place, the writer can then complete the introduction and conclusion paragraphs. After the outside is done, the writer can then fill in the supporting details for the body paragraphs.

4. Microcosm—A microcosm is a miniature world. It captures all of the elements of the big world in a compact example. A microcosm allows us to learn more about the big world by looking at a smaller world within the world. You can apply this idea to your composition by writing one paragraph that captures all the elements of you topic. When finished, you will have a miniature version of your essay. Then, you can add details to expand your miniature essay into a full-sized essay.

5. Whatever Works—Use your imagination to come up with new approaches that work.

III. After Writing

A. Reviewing

When you have finished writing, you have not finished the writing process. You have a first draft—a piece of writing that is finished but not finished.

1. Self-Review—First, you need to look back at your writing, and review it yourself. As you read over what you have written, you need to consider five areas and look for ways to improve your essay in these five areas.

Ideas and Information—Is the information accurate, appropriate, and detailed?
Organization—Does the essay follow the introduction, body, and conclusion framework? Does it use chronology, sequence, or another pattern effectively?
Sentence Structure—Do the sentences meet the requirements of good, complete sentences? Is your grammar correct?
Word Use—Do the words chosen have the appropriate meaning and form? Do they follow the standards of conventional usage?
Punctuation Plus—Is the format, style, and punctuation appropriate?

2. Peer Review—After you have done your best, you should have a classmate, friend, or family member review your essay. Another ESL student should be able to make suggestions about your ideas and organization. He or she may also have knowledge of how to improve your structure, word use, and mechanics. If you have a peer who is a native speaker of English, you can ask her/him for feedback in all five areas.

3. Expert Review—Another valuable option is to get feedback from your professor or from a tutor, especially if your college has a writing center.

B. Finishing

1. Rewriting—After you have feedback from your own review and the review of others, you need to rewrite your essay. If you have a lot of reorganization and rewriting to do, you will want to return to the writing step above and follow those guidelines again. If you have little reorganization and rewriting, you can focus on making the minor changes. After rewriting, you may want to repeat the review step.

2. Proofreading—After rewriting, you should produce a final draft as perfect as you can make it. When you have your final draft, you will need to proofread it. Proofreading involves looking very closely at all the details of your writing to make sure that there are no accidental or overlooked errors. Spelling and punctuation are some of the details to consider.

C. Sharing/Publishing

Once you have proofread and corrected any errors, you are ready to share your writing with its intended audience or publish it for wider distribution.

Related Structures

Transitions of Sequence

Chronological order, which was explored in Chapter 3, is useful when actions or events occur in a specific order in time. A writer can establish specific time frames by using time words or phrases. When writing about a process, the writer needs to establish the order in which the steps of the process occur. What comes first, second, third, and so on? What step comes right after what other step? The order of the steps is always the same no matter when they occur in time, so specific time frames are not important. Instead, the writer wants to focus on the order, or sequence.

Several transitions are available to make the sequence clear. They can be divided into those useful at the beginning, middle, and end of the process.

<u>Beginning</u>
first, initially, at first, to begin with

<u>Middle</u>
second, third, fourth, fifth ....
next, subsequently, then, afterwards

<u>End</u>
finally, last, lastly, ultimately, eventually, in the end

6.4 Exercise / Evaluate

Exercise 1: Warm-up Writing

In a paragraph (10-12 sentences), explain to the reader how to get a driver's license in the place where you are living. Your audience is students new to the area who need to get a driver's license. Your purpose for writing is to inform the new students to help make the process easier for them. Include all the necessary steps in the required order. Explain in detail each step and the actions associated with it. If you have gotten a driver's license, use your experience as a basis for your writing. If you have not gotten a driver's license or if you need more information, you may want to interview someone with experience, or you may want to get more information from the agency that issues driver's licenses. You can also explain how to obtain a driver's license in your country. One way to start is:

A car is a necessity in most American towns and cities, so you will need a driver's license. In order to obtain a driver's license, you need to take several important steps....

OR, if you do not need to drive, explain how to get around without a car.

Fortunately, in this city, students do not need a car to get around. However, preparation is still important to assure that they can easily, safely, and inexpensively get to where they need to go....

Exercise 2: Skill / Structure Practice

A. Organizing by sequence. Statisticians, scientists, social scientists and others use the following processes to organize and make sense of data. The steps listed here are not in the correct order. Put them in the correct order. (There may be more than one answer possible.) Use the number 1 for the first step, 2 for the second, and so on. If you are not familiar with statistics, ask a classmate for an explanation of these processes, or consult a mathematics book.

Calculating the Mean (the average)

_____divide the sum by the number of values added
_____collect the values to be averaged and count the number of values
_____add all of the values together (sum)

Finding the Median (the middle value)

_____using this midpoint number as a guide, find the middle value, the one with an equal number of values before and after it
_____(b) calculate the middle value by averaging the two values on either side of the midpoint
_____count the number of values and divide the number of values by two to determine the midpoint of the number of values
_____collect the values to be averaged and arrange the values from least to greatest
_____(a) the middle value will be at the center of the list
_____if the number of values is odd, see (a) and if the number of values is even, see (b)

Calculating the Standard Deviation

_____calculate the square root of the variance
_____multiply each deviation by itself (square the deviations)
_____calculate the mean of a group of values
_____calculate the mean of the group of squared deviations (variance)
_____find the difference between each value and the mean (the deviation)

B. Using the information from Part A above, describe each process in paragraph form. Use sequence words appropriately to make the order clear to the reader. Put verbs in the appropriate form and tense.

1. Your first paragraph should use the imperative form. You may want to begin something like this:

Organizing and making sense of data is a valuable skill. One way to analyze data is to calculate the mean of the values. In order to calculate the mean, follow these steps....

2. Your second paragraph should use "you" as its subject. You may want to begin something like this:

> No matter what discipline you study or career you choose, you will probably need to know how to organize and make sense of data. If you need to analyze a group of values in a useful way, especially when you have a few unusually high or low values, you can find the median. To find the median, you take these steps....

3. Your third paragraph should use "statisticians" and "they" as its subjects. You may want to begin something like this:

> Statisticians use a variety of tools to organize and analyze data. When they need to establish how values in a group differ from the mean, these mathematicians calculate the standard deviation. Statisticians calculating the standard deviation employ the following process....

C. Put the following verbs and sequence words in the appropriate blanks in the process paragraph below. One of the words will not be needed. Remember to put the verbs in the appropriate form to match their subject.

analyze	ask	be	come	eventually
first	form	make	next	predict
prove	read	second	then	use

The Scientific Method

A scientist, like the two-time Nobel Prize winner Marie Curie, _____ the scientific method to investigate and prove why things are as they are. There are several steps in the scientific method. _____, the scientist _____ observations of things that occur in nature. _____, she _____ questions about why these things occur. _____, she _____ a hypothesis (an educated guess) to try to answer her questions. Based on the hypothesis, the scientist _____ what should happen if the hypothesis is correct. _____, she designs an experiment to test the hypothesis. She _____ the results of the experiment to see if the predictions have come true. If the predictions _____ verified (or come true), she concludes that the hypothesis is correct. If the predictions _____ not_____ true, she modifies her hypothesis and repeats. _____, if she _____ enough hypotheses, she can establish a theory of how things work.

Exercise 3: Focused Writing Practice

The following notes give an idea of how someone with experience buys a used car. Use these notes to write about the used-car-buying process. Write grammatically correct complete sentences. Be sure that every sentence has a subject and verb and that they agree. To make things simpler, use "experienced used car buyers," "buyers," "they," and similar words as your subjects. Put your sentences together into well-organized paragraphs. You will need to add sequence words where necessary. You will also need to combine some ideas together into compound and complex sentences. You should use almost all of the details provided in the notes. You may, however, decide to leave out a few facts if you find they are not important steps in the process.

Notes about used car buying

- assess needs
- determine amount feasible to spend monthly for the car, its insurance, and its operation
- find out from the DMV the laws related to buying and selling used cars
- find tips on buying quality used cars
- decide on a type of car that meets needs and fits budget
- find information about the best models and years in the type chosen
- look in the newspaper, shopper's guides, and online sources for the cars available
- look at offerings from new car dealers, used car dealers (large and small), auctions, and private sellers
- note the range of years and prices offered
- arrange to see a group of cars
- ask private sellers why they are selling
- ask for a history of the car—maintenance, mileage, emissions test, accident records
- inspect personally, outside, inside, and under hood
- use a checklist from tips on buying quality used cars
- turn on the engine
- watch and listen to the engine for anything unusual
- while the engine is running check gauges and warning lights
- turn on everything to be sure that it works
- test drive the car
- pay careful attention to how the car operates under a variety of conditions
- have the car inspected by a qualified mechanic
- determine if everything meets with approval
- make an offer lower than you are willing to pay
- explain that you have researched the going rates
- negotiate
- if the asking price is too high, leave with a promise to contact later
- if the price is acceptable, complete the deal
- follow the applicable laws
- pay in cash or cashier's check
- receive the title or temporary substitute
- assure that title, tags, and insurance is in order

Exercise 4: Process Writing Assignment

This assignment will give you practice writing about a process. Process writing describes how to do something, how to make something, or how something works. It is the type of writing used in demonstrations, directions, and instructions. It is also used in writing about scientific experiments and social science studies. Directions and instructions are typically written with present tense verbs. Other processes may be described with present or past tense verbs (or occasionally with future tense verbs), whichever is appropriate to the context. Process writing may use third person nouns and pronouns (he, she, it, they) as subjects for a general, impersonal feel. It may use the second person pronoun (you) for a more specific, personal feel. And, it may use the imperative verb form to give a direct, immediate feel.

Studying in a Foreign Country. Using the information that you and your classmates brainstormed and sequenced in the "Engage" activity for this chapter, write three to five paragraphs to explain in detail the steps that a student must take to successfully study in a foreign country.   Your audience is students who are interested in studying in a foreign country in the future. Your purpose is to inform these students so that they "get off on the right foot."

1. In your first paragraph (the introduction), give an overview of why students might want to study in a foreign country. Include some of the key benefits of studying abroad.

2. In your middle paragraphs (the body), use your sequence of the seven to ten steps from the "Engage" activity to detail the steps that students should follow to successfully study in a foreign country. Write complete sentences that are connected together into good paragraphs. Use transitions of sequence to make the order clear. DO NOT just list the steps. The goal is to write sentences and paragraphs.

3. In your last paragraph (the conclusion), summarize the benefits of studying abroad and the importance of following a systematic process.

Self-Review. After you have written your process paper, complete the following "Quick Self-Review Sheet." This sheet will quickly give you an idea of how well you have focused on the assignment and included the important elements of an essay. It will also suggest some improvements you can make on your own before you share your essay with anyone else.

Quick Self-Review Sheet

Your name: _____   Audience: _____

Professor's name: _____   Purpose: _____

Course name: _____   Essay type: <u>Process</u>

Date: _____   Source: _____

Title: _____

Answer the following questions with yes or no. If you answer no, make the additions or changes necessary to answer yes.

General

1. Does the essay have a title?

2. Is the audience for the essay clear?

3. Is the purpose for the essay clear?

4. Does the essay describe a process (a sequence of steps)?

Introduction

5. Does the essay have an introductory paragraph?

6. Does the essay have an invitation to attract the interest of the audience?

7. Does the essay have a thesis statement—one complete sentence that clearly states the main idea?

8. Does the thesis statement focus on a specific idea?

Body

9. Are the points that support the thesis developed in detail?

10. Do the supporting points clearly connect with the thesis?

11. Are there enough supporting points?

12. Does the body of the essay include firm evidence?

13. Is the evidence adequate to convince the readers?

Conclusion

14. Is there a concluding paragraph?

15. Does the conclusion include at least one: a restatement of the thesis; a summary of the main points; a call to action?

16. Does the paper give a feeling of completeness?

Structure, Word Use, and Mechanics

17. Have you carefully checked the grammar and vocabulary to avoid as many mistakes as possible?

Plan for Second Draft

18. What questions need to be answered before the next draft? What changes need to be made?

(See the "Extra" chapter at the end of the book for additional copies of this sheet.)

Peer Review. Share your completed process writing with one of your classmates. Have her/him respond to your first draft by answering the following questions on a separate sheet of paper:

<u>Peer Response</u>

1. Write three things that you found interesting about your classmate's essay.

2. Write three questions that you have now that you have read your classmate's essay.

3. Write three suggestions that you have for your classmate to incorporate into her/his next draft.

Expert Review. Share your draft with a native speaker who is an experienced writer—a peer at your college, a tutor, a writing-center instructor, or your writing professor. Ask for specific feedback about questions and concerns that you have about your paper. Your final draft will be evaluated on the areas listed in the "Evaluation" section below, so be sure to identify the areas and specific points with which you need the most help.

Evaluation

As you review and revise your essay, keep in mind that your writing will be evaluated on:

Ideas and Information—Is it detailed and specific enough to help the reader?
Organization—Does your first paragraph introduce the idea, your middle paragraphs explain it, and your last paragraph review the idea?
Sentence Structure—Do you have complete sentences with correct verb tenses?
Word Use—Do you use content words appropriately?
Punctuation Plus—Are your paragraphs indented? Do you have capital letters at the beginning of each sentence and full stops at the end?

6.5 Extend

Beyond the Classroom—Write out two of your favorite recipes to share with your classmates. Be sure to include the necessary ingredients, the amount of each, and the steps required to complete the recipe. Also, explain how the dish should be served and eaten and if it should accompany other dishes.

Putting It All Together—Find a scholarly journal article in your library (or available online) on the topic of international students or learning a second language. These articles describe social science research studies. OR, find an article in a scientific journal that describes an experiment. Look at the titles and headings used to organize the article. Make an outline of the parts of the journal article. Don't worry about the content. Just focus on the steps that the writer followed in the article.

Thinking Skills—Search the Internet for sites on how to use the scientific method or how to write a journal article. Find three or four different sources. Use your sources to write a summary of the process you have chosen.

Chapter 7—Description

This chapter applies the essay-writing process to descriptive writing. Description essays are useful in many contexts. Descriptive writing is the basis of many other forms of writing.

7.1 Engage—Spend Your Next Vacation with Us

The purpose of this activity is to use what you already know and to practice describing people, places, and/or things in appropriate detail.

Tourism is a very important part of the economies of most countries. Americans spend a lot of money each year visiting their own country and others. You have been asked to develop an advertising campaign, brochure, and a Web page to encourage Americans to visit your native country. You will want to include all of the important information that Americans will need while traveling to your country and visiting interesting sites.

Forming Groups: Students should divide into groups of three or four using one of the grouping methods from a previous chapter.

1. What information should you include and highlight in your advertising campaign? In your group, decide the type of information that should be included in brochures and Web sites. Make lists of the categories of information that should be included in a brochure, in a Web site, and in both. (Use 15 minutes.)

2. In your groups, decide how the information should be organized. What should come first, second, next, and so on? Revise your list to show the order that you would use to organize the information. (Use 10 minutes.)

3. Individually, write down the details that you know about your country in the categories that you have decided upon and organized. Try to include as much as you can in the appropriate categories. Also, come up with a slogan—a phrase or sentence—to catch people's interest. (Use 20 minutes.)

4. Back in your group, have each person take five minutes to present his or her slogan and explain the important details. The listeners should ask questions and make suggestions after each presentation. (Use 15 to 20 minutes.)

5. For homework, create a brochure to encourage American tourists to visit your country and provide information that they will find useful on their trip.

7.2 Explore—Types of Descriptive Writing: Travel Writing

In your groups, you decided what kinds of information should be included in a travel brochure and Web site. Travel guides and Web sites are very common. These sources provide travelers with information that they need to enjoy their trips. Another type of writing related to travel is called travel writing or adventure writing. In these narratives, writers share stories about their travels. Readers can enjoy the experience of traveling without leaving their homes. Libraries, bookstores, and online sources have many interesting sources for people interested in traveling and for people who want to learn about others' travels.

Libraries

Reference Books—Libraries have encyclopedias, atlases, almanacs, and gazetteers that contain information about places.
Books—Libraries also contain travel guides, geography books, and essays and books by travelers.
Periodicals—Popular magazines such as *Conde Nast Traveler*, *National Geographic Traveler*, *Time Out*, and *Travel and Leisure* include articles that provide tourist guides and articles in which travelers share their experiences.

Bookstores

Books and Periodicals—Bookstores have special sections full of travel guides, geography books, and travel writing and also sell the popular magazines that explore interesting places.

Online

Use your favorite search engine to find travel guides, geography sources, and travel writing available on the Internet. Just type in travel guides OR travel writing OR the name of the place you are interested in on the search line and visit the sites highlighted.

Activity

1. Find examples of each of the sources for travel information listed above. You will need to visit a library or bookstore and use the Internet. Use the information you gather to complete Table 7.1.

Table 7.1—Travel Information Sources

Type	Name of source	Where did you find it?	Subject of the source	Why is the place interesting?
Reference book				
Book				
Magazine				
Web site				

2. Find two different types of sources with information related to your country. Use these sources to fill in details about your country and add them to the brochure or Web site you developed in the "Engage" activity. List the sources that you used in your brochure or Web site as sources your readers can use to find more information.

7.3 Explain—Description Essays

For people to notice the world around them is natural. Every day, they see other people, places, and things, and they note their characteristics. Having made these observations, people often want to share them with others. Such descriptions are common.

A **description essay** allows a writer to share what he or she has noticed. As the name suggests, this type of essay is used to describe a person, place, or thing. These are concrete, tangible (touchable) topics. (With abstract, intangible things, ideas, or concepts, writers can write what is called a definition essay.)

Good descriptions use a lot of sensory details. They require the writer to explore sight, sound, smell, taste, and touch. Good descriptions use words to create a detailed image of the subject in the mind of the reader. They make the person, place, or thing come alive for the reader.

John Muir (1838-1914), an American naturalist and conservationist, wrote the following description of the Yosemite Valley, now part of one of the United States' national parks.

> No temple made with hands can compare with Yosemite. Every rock in its walls seems to glow with life. Some lean back in majestic repose; others, absolutely sheer or nearly so for thousands of feet, advance beyond their companions in thoughtful attitudes, giving welcome to storms and calms alike, seemingly aware, yet heedless, of everything going on about them. Awful in stern, immovable majesty, how softly these rocks are adorned, and how fine and reassuring the company they keep: their feet among beautiful groves and meadows, their brows in the sky, a thousand flowers leaning confidingly against their feet, bathed in floods of water, floods of light, while the snow and waterfalls, the winds and avalanches and clouds shine and sing and wreathe about them as the years go by, and myriads of small winged creatures—birds, bees, butterflies—give glad animation and help to make all the air into music. Down through the middle of the Valley flows the crystal Merced, River of Mercy, peacefully quiet, reflecting lilies and trees and the onlooking rocks; things frail and fleeting and types of endurance meeting here and blending in countless forms, as if into this one mountain mansion Nature had gathered her choicest treasures, to draw her lovers into close and confiding communion with her.

John Muir—*The Yosemite*, 1912

Related Structures

Descriptive Words

One way a writer can create a detailed image of the subject being described is to use descriptive words, phrases, and clauses.

Nouns

As was discussed in Chapter 1, a noun—a person, place, thing, or concept—can be common or proper. Proper nouns are specific names for people, places, or things. Common nouns, on the other hand, can be quite general. For example: a man, an animal, a plant, a vehicle, or music. Nonetheless, some common nouns are more specific and quite descriptive. Writers who want to make their writing richer in description should try to use these more specific, descriptive nouns.

In the examples that follow, the most general noun is at the top of each group. Those that follow are more specific and descriptive.

a man
a blond
a doctor, a cardiologist
a politician, a socialist
a helper, a philanthropist

an animal
a carnivore, a predator
a mammal, a marsupial
a horse, a mare, a yearling, a pinto
a cat, a kitten, a tabby

a plant
a flower, a rose
a bush, a shrub, a tree
a conifer, a pine

a vehicle
a car, a coupe, a sedan, a convertible
a truck, a van, a minivan
a boat, a sailboat, a sloop

music
blues, folk, jazz, polka, rock, soul
a ballad, a march, a fugue, a symphony
an overture, a sonata, a finale

Adjectives

Adjectives are words used to describe or give more information about nouns. Adjectives provide many different types of information about the nouns that they describe. The main categories of adjectives are:

Evaluation—amazing/boring, beautiful/ugly, delicious/disgusting ...
Size—big, immense, tall, tiny, wide ...
Age—ancient, futuristic, new, nineteenth-century, old ...
Shape—oval, pointed, round, square, triangular ...
Condition—broken, cracked, torn, whole ...
Action—bouncing, falling, oscillating, pulsating ...
Color—black, blue, green, orange, red, turquoise, white, yellow ...
Origin—African, Celtic, Hispanic, Swiss, Texan, Vietnamese ...
Ideology—Buddhist, communist, democratic, Muslim ...
Material—aluminum, chocolate, cotton, plastic, wooden ...

Adjectives typically come before the noun that they describe.

young men   tall buildings   brown sugar   economic assistance

Adjectives may come after the noun that they describe when they are connected to the noun by the verb <u>be</u> (in all of its forms) or one of the other linking verbs in the following lists.

<u>Sensory linking verbs</u>
look, appear
sound
taste
feel, seem
smell

<u>Change in status linking verbs</u>
become
grow
remain
turn

Examples:
The man <u>sounded</u> frightened.
The food <u>smelled</u> delicious.
The light <u>turned</u> green.

Other Words Used to Describe Nouns

1. Determiners

Determiners are another group of words that describe or give more information about nouns. They include:

Words that define which one:
Articles—an, an, the
Demonstratives—this, that, these, those
Possessives—my, your, his, her, its, our, their, _____'s (for singular nouns), _____s' (for plural nouns)

Words that describe how many:
Non-specific quantifiers—all, any, both, a couple (= approximately 2), each, either, every, few (= not many), a few (= between 3 and several), little (= not much), a little (= a small amount), a lot of (= many), many, much, neither, a number of (= many), several, some
Numbers—one, two, three, four, five...

Words that establish order:
Ordinals—first, second, third, fourth, fifth...

2. Other Nouns

Nouns are often used to describe other nouns to specify type, style, or purpose. For example:

law student   tax form   beach vacation   desert sky

Descriptive Phrases and Clauses

Adjective Clauses

Often more than one word is used to describe a single noun. A group of words that share a related function is called a phrase, so a group of words that describe a noun is called an adjective phrase. In English, the order of the words used in adjective phrases is important. The following order is not always perfect, but it should offer a guide for how to order adjectives and other modifiers when you are using more than one to describe a noun.

Guide to Ordering Adjectives and Other Modifiers

Read down for order.

Determiners					
which one	the	|	that	his	my
how many	|	many	|	|	three
order	|	|	|	first	|
Evaluation	eerie	delicious	terrible	|	wonderful
Size	|	large	|	|	big
Age	|	|	old	|	new
Shape	|	|	|	|	oval
Condition	|	|	broken-down	|	|
Action	flickering	|	|	|	|
Color	purple	|	blue	|	red
Origin	|	Swiss	Ford	|	|
Ideology	|	|	|	|	|
Material	|	|	|	woolen	cotton
Noun used as adjective	|	|	|	hunting	prayer
Noun being described	light	chocolates	tractor	cap	rugs

... the eerie flickering purple light ...

... many delicious large Swiss chocolates ...

...that terrible old broken-down blue Ford tractor ...

... his first woolen hunting cap ...

... my three wonderful big new oval red cotton prayer rugs ...

When two adjectives from the same category are used in an adjective phrase, they can be used in either order and should be separated by "and" or a comma.

... many delicious, beautiful French pastries ... OR ... many beautiful, delicious French pastries ...

Prepositional Phrases

A prepositional phrase (a preposition + a noun phrase) can also be used to describe a noun. Prepositional phrases typically come immediately after the nouns that they describe. Occasionally, they come just before the noun. Prepositional phrases often add details about the noun in terms of place, time, and type.

the visitors from Pakistan	the building at the end of the lane
the meeting at nine o'clock	the snowstorm during the Christmas holiday
a man of his word	a course in chemistry

In some cases, you can use either adjectives or prepositional phrases to describe a noun. In other cases, either the adjective OR the prepositional phrase is the preferred way to describe the noun.

The Liberty Bell is in Philadelphia.
("Liberty" is a noun used as an adjective to describe the bell.)

The Statue of Liberty is in New York.
("Liberty" is the object of the preposition, or the noun of a prepositional phrase. "Of liberty," the prepositional phrase, describes which statue.)

Adjective Clauses

Remember that clauses are groups of words with their own subject and verb (with time—past, present, or future). A clause that is used to describe a noun is an adjective clause. Adjective clauses typically come immediately after the noun that they describe. Adjective clause markers are the wh- question words below.

<u>People</u>
who—substitutes for noun subjects and pronoun subject forms (I, you, he, she, we, and they)
whom—substitutes for noun objects and pronoun object forms (me, you, him, her, us, them)
whose—substitutes for noun and pronoun possessive adjectives (my, your, his, her, our, their)

<u>Things</u>
that (instead of what)—substitutes for noun subjects and objects and for the word "it"
which (instead of what)—substitutes for noun subjects and objects and for the word "it"

<u>Times</u>
when—substitutes for noun subjects and objects related to time

<u>Places</u>
where—substitutes for noun subjects and objects related to place

Combining Sentences by Using Adjective Clauses

Adjective clauses allow you to give more information about nouns in your sentences. But even more important, they allow you to combine two or more sentences into one longer, more complex sentence. Using complex sentences along with simple and compound sentences gives variety to your writing. It also gives the writing a more formal, developed quality.

Creating complex sentences can also lead to problems and mistakes. These mistakes may involve including unnecessary words or putting the adjective clause in the wrong place. The examples below follow a step-by-step approach to creating adjective clauses to help you avoid some potential mistakes.

A. Combining Two Sentences with Related Subjects

<u>People</u>

Step 1: Write your ideas in complete sentences.
Idea/sentence #1: <u>The author</u> influenced many twentieth-century American mystery writers.
Idea/sentence #2: <u>The author</u> was one of the first writers to write detective stories.

Step 2: Substitute the appropriate pronoun for the shared words in the second sentence.
<u>The author</u> influenced many twentieth-century American mystery writers.
<u>He</u> was one of the first writers to write detective stories.

Step 3: Combine the sentences by inserting the second sentence after the words referred to by the pronoun.
The author <u>he was one of the first writers to write detective stories</u> influenced many twentieth-century American mystery writers.

Step 4: Substitute the adjective clause marker for the pronoun to create an adjective clause.
The author <u>who was one of the first writers to write detective stories</u> influenced many twentieth-century American mystery writers. (*Who* serves as the subject of the adjective clause.)

<u>Things</u>

Step 1: Write your ideas in complete sentences.
Idea/sentence #1: <u>The movie</u> was filmed on location in my home country.
Idea/sentence #2: <u>The movie</u> won the Academy Award for best foreign language picture.

Step 2: Substitute the appropriate pronoun for the shared words in the second sentence.
<u>The movie</u> was filmed on location in my home country.
<u>It</u> won the Academy Award for best foreign language picture.

Step 3: Combine the sentences by inserting the second sentence after the words referred to by the pronoun.
The movie <u>it won the Academy Award for best foreign language picture</u> was filmed on location in my home country.

Step 4: Substitute the adjective clause marker for the pronoun to create an adjective clause.
The movie <u>that won the Academy Award for best foreign language picture</u> was filmed on location in my home country. (*That* serves as the subject of the adjective clause.)

2. Combining Two Sentences with Related Subject and Object or Related Object and Object

<u>People</u>

Step 1: Write your ideas in complete sentences.
Idea/sentence #1: <u>The painter</u> is having a special exhibition of his works at Gallery Five.
Idea/sentence #2: We met <u>the painter</u> at Frank's party.

Step 2: Substitute the appropriate pronoun for the shared words in the second sentence.
<u>The painter</u> is having a special exhibition of his works at Gallery Five.
We met <u>him</u> at Frank's party.

Step 3: Move the pronoun to the beginning of the second sentence.
<u>The painter</u> is having a special exhibition of his works at Gallery Five.
<u>him</u> we met at Frank's party.

Step 4: Combine the sentences by inserting the second sentence after the words referred to by the pronoun.
The painter <u>him we met at Frank's party</u> is having a special exhibition of his works at Gallery Five.

Step 5: Substitute the adjective clause marker for the pronoun to create an adjective clause.
The painter <u>whom we met at Frank's party</u> is having a special exhibition of his works at Gallery Five. (*Whom* serves as the object of the adjective clause.)

<u>Things</u>

Step 1: Write your ideas in complete sentences.
Idea/sentence #1: The home team won <u>the basketball game</u>.
Idea/sentence #2: We watched <u>the basketball game</u> on television at the sports bar.

Step 2: Substitute the appropriate pronoun for the shared words in the second sentence.
The home team won <u>the basketball game</u>.
We watched <u>it</u> on television at the sports bar.

Step 3: Move the pronoun to the beginning of the second sentence.
The home team won <u>the basketball game</u>.
<u>it</u> we watched on television at the sports bar.

Step 4: Combine the sentences by inserting the second sentence after the words referred to by the pronoun.
The home team won the basketball game <u>it we watched on television at the sports bar</u>.

Step 5: Substitute the adjective clause marker for the pronoun to create an adjective clause.
The home team won the basketball game that we watched on television at the sports bar. (*That* serves as the object of the adjective clause.)

Times

Step 1: Write your ideas in complete sentences.
Idea/sentence #1: Tourism in Georgia increased during the summer.
Idea/sentence #2: The Olympic Games were held in Atlanta during the summer.

Step 2: Substitute the appropriate pronoun for the shared words in the second sentence.
Tourism in Georgia increased during the summer.
The Olympic Games were held in Atlanta then.

Step 3: Move the pronoun to the beginning of the second sentence.
Tourism in Georgia increased during the summer.
then the Olympic Games were held in Atlanta.

Step 4: Combine the sentences by inserting the second sentence after the words referred to by the pronoun.
Tourism in Georgia increased during the summer then the Olympic Games were held in Atlanta.

Step 5: Substitute the adjective clause marker for the pronoun to create an adjective clause.
Tourism in Georgia increased during the summer when the Olympic Games were held in Atlanta. (*When* serves as the object of the adjective clause.)

Places

Step 1: Write your ideas in complete sentences.
Idea/sentence #1: The bicycle shop was moved to the Henry Ford Museum in Michigan.
Idea/sentence #2: The Wright Brothers designed their first airplanes in the bicycle shop.

Step 2: Substitute the appropriate pronoun for the similar words in the second sentence.
The bicycle shop was moved to the Henry Ford Museum in Michigan.
The Wright Brothers designed their first airplanes there. (The preposition *in* is deleted.)

Step 3: Move the pronoun to the beginning of the second sentence.
The bicycle shop was moved to the Henry Ford Museum in Michigan.
there the Wright Brothers designed their first airplanes.

Step 4: Combine the sentences by inserting the second sentence after the words referred to by the pronoun.
The bicycle shop there the Wright Brothers designed their first airplanes was moved to the Henry Ford Museum in Michigan.

Step 5: Substitute the adjective clause marker for the pronoun to create an adjective clause. The bicycle shop <u>where the Wright Brothers designed their first airplanes</u> was moved to the Henry Ford Museum in Michigan. (*Where* serves as the object of the adjective clause.)

C. Combining Two Sentences with Related Subject and Possessive

Step 1: Write your ideas in complete sentences.
Idea/sentence #1: <u>The singer</u> was injured in an automobile accident.
Idea/sentence #2: <u>The singer'</u>s new CD was just released.

Step 2: Substitute the appropriate pronoun for the similar words in the second sentence.
<u>The singer</u> was injured in an automobile accident.
<u>His</u> new CD was just released.

Step 3: Combine the sentences by inserting the second sentence after the words referred to by the pronoun.
The singer <u>his new CD was just released</u> was injured in an automobile accident.

Step 4: Substitute the adjective clause marker for the pronoun to create an adjective clause.
The singer <u>whose new CD was just released</u> was injured in an automobile accident. (*Whose* is a possessive form connected to the noun that follows it.)

7.4 Exercise / Evaluate

Exercise 1: Warm-up Writing

For this activity, you will need a partner. You are each going to describe the clothing of the other in a paragraph of 10-12 sentences. Be descriptive, not judgmental. When you describe someone's clothing, you can include physical details of the clothing, a characterization of the style and who typically wears that style, and what the clothing suggests about the person wearing it. Include all of these elements in your description. Also, try to make your writing rich with adjectives and other noun modifiers. Use the list in Exercise 2 below to remind you of the type of adjectives you should use.

Exercise 2: Related Structure/Skills

A. Using Adjectives to Describe. Take a sheet of paper and fold the right and left sides together to make two columns each running from top to bottom. Repeat for each column, making a total of four columns. Now, fold the top and bottom together to divide the paper and your columns in half. You should now have eight tall boxes on each side of the paper. At the top of each box, write one of the categories from the list below. You will have to use the back of the paper also.

Under each category of describing words, list ten words that fit the category. You may want to use a dictionary or thesaurus to get ideas.

Determiners
       which one—
       how many—
       order—
Evaluation—
Size—
Age—
Shape—
Condition—
Action—
Color—
Origin—
Ideology—
Material—
Noun used as adjective—
Noun—

B. Use your list from Exercise 2A above and write 10 descriptive sentences that each include adjectives in the appropriate order.

C. Using a Variety of Forms to Describe. English allows you to add descriptive details by using a variety of forms. Provide more specific detail about each of the following nouns by using a descriptive noun, using the noun with an adjective, using the noun with a prepositional phrase, and using the noun with an adjective clause. For example:

a man, a blond, a blond man, a man with blond hair, a man who has blond hair
a city, a metropolis, a large city, a city with many people, a city that has a large population

a book—

a building—

culture—

entertainment—

food—

land—

a leader—

a mountain—

a pastime—

a school—

D. Combining Sentences. Combine each of the following groups of sentences into one grammatically correct sentence.

1. Brazil has a diverse population.
Brazil's population is made up of the descendants of European immigrants, Africans brought for slave labor, and peoples indigenous to South America.

2. In 221 B.C., the King of Qin united many small Chinese states into one empire.
The King of Qin's name was Ying Zheng.

3. *Metropolis* was one of the first masterpieces of science-fiction film.
Fritz Lang made *Metropolis* in 1927 in Germany.

4. Cairo was a city of approximately a quarter of a million people in 1798.
Napoleon Bonaparte's French armies invaded Cairo in 1798.

5. Construction workers found previously unknown Greek historical sites.
The construction workers were preparing venues for the 2004 Olympic Games in Athens.

6. The Tatra Range contains the highest peaks in the Carpathian Mountains.
The people of Poland and Slovakia enjoy the Tatra Range for skiing and other alpine sports.

7. The Aztec people had an advanced civilization with a beautiful capital city at Tenochtitlan.
Spanish explorers first encountered the Aztec people in 1519.

8. Ferdinand Magellan was killed during a battle between local Philippine groups in 1521. Magellan's expedition completed the first single-voyage circumnavigation of the earth.

9. Pakistan was founded in 1947.
Karachi became the capital of Pakistan in 1947.
Karachi is a busy port on the Arabian Sea.

10. The empire of Kanem grew powerful in the 11th century through textile and mineral trade. The empire of Kanem was in north-central Africa.
The countries of Libya, Chad, Niger, and Nigeria are now located in north-central Africa.

Exercise 3: Focused Writing Practice

The following description lacks details. Rewrite it using much more descriptive language. Use descriptive nouns, adjectives, prepositional phrases, and adjective clauses to capture the sensory (sight, sound, smell, taste, and touch) and other details of the scene. Make the moment come alive for the reader. Because the scene is not real, you can use your experience and imagination to fill in the details.

Last night, I was walking along the street near the campus. As I came to a corner, I saw a person sitting at an outdoor table. I could not believe my eyes, but I thought I saw someone I had known all of my life. It seemed impossible that I would see that person here, but I felt sure that this was that person. I felt confident that this was, in fact, this person, because what I now saw before my eyes fit perfectly with my memory....

Exercise 4: Description Essay Assignment

This assignment will give you practice writing a description essay. Descriptive writing captures a person, place, or thing with vivid details and shares these details with the reader. It is the type of writing used in personal portraits and fictional character sketches, travel information, and object specifications. Descriptions focused on living people and current observations are typically written with present tense verbs. Descriptions focused on subjects from the past or future may use past tense verbs or future tense verbs respectively, whichever is appropriate to the context. Descriptive writing typically uses third person nouns and pronouns (he, she, it, they) as grammatical subjects.

Describing Your Hometown or Home Country. Using the lists and details that you and your classmates created in the Engage activity for this chapter, write five to seven paragraphs to describe in detail the features of your hometown or country that a tourist would find interesting. Your audience is people who are interested in visiting your hometown or country. Your purpose is to provide these people with information useful to them during their travels.

Using the Writing Process

Follow the steps of the writing process spelled out below to complete your description.

I. Before Writing

A. Getting Ideas—Focused Listing

Look over the lists and details you created with your classmates in the "Engage" activity. Do your details include observations from all of your senses? Fill in the columns in the "Description Template" (Table 7.2) with the details that best characterize your hometown or home country.

Table 7.2—Description Template

sight	sound	smell	taste	touch	other feelings

B. Grouping Ideas

Travel writing often includes information in a number of categories (classifications). Decide which of these categories or others you would like to use and their order in your essay.

Climate
Culture
Economy
History
Land
Location
Points of interest

Popular activities
Population
Society
Transportation
Other

II. During Writing

A. Planning

Now that you have ideas for your essay, you need to plan the writing. Answer these questions to help you.

1. Establishing the Writing Context

Whom do you want to read your writing? (Audience)
What are you writing? (Form)
When and where will you write? When and where is the description set? (Setting)
Why are you writing? (Purpose)
How will you write? (Process)
Which sources will you use? (Source)

2. Formulating a Main Idea—Write your working thesis statement. (It is all right if you decide to change it later.)

3. Developing Support—Be sure to use objective evidence with the subjective evidence.

4. Organizing

a. Outlining

Use an outline to plan the parts of your essay's body. See Chapter 4 for a reminder of outlining.

B. Writing

Body

Use the body-first technique for writing. (See Chapter 6 for a reminder of this technique.) Use the outline that you created above to help guide you. Write your topic sentences first and then fill in the details necessary to support the topic sentences.

Introduction

Write an introduction to fit the body that you have already written. Begin with an invitation that catches the attention of the readers and convinces them that they want to learn more about your hometown or home country. Provide enough orientation to prepare the readers for your thesis statement—your main idea. If you need to make changes to your thesis statement so that it better fits the body that you have written, make the changes now.

Conclusion

Write a conclusion that fits with the body and introduction that you have already written. Include a transition sentence, a review of the important ideas from your body and/or a restatement of your thesis, as well as a resolution. Recommend action that the readers can take to prepare to visit your hometown or country.

Bringing It All Together—Put your introduction, body, and conclusion together in the appropriate order. Read it over to assure that you have utilized the six elements of good paragraph and essay development—topic, focus, support, logic, unity, and coherence. (See Chapter 2 for a review of these elements.) For this essay, pay special attention to your coherence. Consider your transition words and your use of repeated words and grammatical structures. Make changes or additions to improve the connectedness of the pieces of your essay.

III. After Writing

A. Reviewing

1. Self-Review. It is important for a writer to look over his or her writing to address any problems before sharing it with someone else. In the previous chapter, you used the "Quick Self-Review Sheet." That is a good tool, but it does not require the writer to examine the writing in very much depth. This time, after you have written your description essay, complete the following sheet, "Responding to a First Draft," to make sure that you have focused on the assignment and included all the appropriate elements of a good paper. Try to answer the questions in as much detail as you can. The purpose of the sheet is to help you focus on what you are doing and encourage you to take responsibility for your own work. Some of the items on the sheet will be explained in more detail later, but do your best to make the paper as effective as you can.

Responding to a First Draft

Answer the following questions with as much detail as you can. Answering these questions will require you to show that you understand what is being done in the paper.

General

1. What is the title? It should give an idea of the main idea of the paper.

2. Who is the main intended audience? Who should read this essay? Check one.

_____General readers _____Specific groups _____Experts
_____The writer's peers _____One specific person _____The writer her/himself

3. What is the main purpose? (check one)

_____Share or Express _____Inform or Explain _____Prove or Persuade

4. What form is used primarily? (check one)

___Narrative ___Process ___Classification and Division
___Description ___Comparison and Contrast ___Evaluation
___Cause and Effect ___Problem and Solution

Introduction

5. Does the paper have an introductory paragraph? If not, how is the reader oriented to the information presented?

6. The Invitation. How is the reader's interest in this paper attracted? (check one)

___a funny story ___a difficult question ___a famous quotation
___a challenge ___a similar or different experience ___something new
___something old in a new light ___a statement of general interest

7. What is the thesis statement? (main idea sentence)

8. How was the general topic focused? (Check all that apply.)

___time ___place ___number or sequence ___category or characteristic
___similarity/difference ___quality ___cause/effect ___problem/solution

Body

9. What are the three to five main points developed in the body of the paper?

10. Do they support the thesis statement? How?

11. Are there points that could be added or removed? What are they?

12. What forms of evidence have been used? (Check all that apply.)
___facts and statistics ___observations ___records ___expert testimony
___precedents ___analogies ___experience ___opinions

13. Is the evidence adequate to convince the readers? If not, what should be done?

Conclusion

14. Is there a concluding paragraph? If not, how is the reader reminded of the key points?

15. Which of the following is included in the conclusion? (Check all that apply.)
_____a restatement of thesis _____a summary of main points
_____a famous quotation related to thesis _____a call to action

16. Does the paper give a feeling of completeness? If not, what is missing, and what should be done?

Sentence Structure, Word Use, and Punctuation

17. Carefully check each of the following items to assure that as many mistakes as possible have been corrected.
___complete sentences ___appropriate verb tenses ___uses transitions
___subject/verb agreement ___correct word forms ___spelling
___correct word order ___capitals and full stops ___format
___modifiers correctly located

Plan for Second Draft

18. What questions need to be answered before the next draft? What changes need to be made?

III. After Writing (continued)

A. Reviewing

2. Peer Review. Share your completed description essay with one of your classmates. Have her/him respond to your first draft by writing the following on a separate sheet of paper:

Peer Response

a. Write three things that you found interesting about your classmate's paper.

b. Write three questions that you have now that you have read your classmate's paper.

c. Write three suggestions that you have for your classmate to incorporate into her/his next draft.

3. Expert Review. Share your draft with a native speaker who is an experienced writer—a peer at your college, a tutor, a writing-center instructor, or your writing professor. Ask for specific feedback about questions and concerns that you have about your paper. Your final draft will be evaluated on the areas listed in the "Evaluation" section below, so be sure to identify the areas and specific points with which you need the most help.

B. Finishing

1. Rewriting—After you have feedback from you own review and the review of others, you need to rewrite your essay. If you have a lot of reorganization and rewriting to do, you will want to return to the writing step above and follow those guidelines again. If you have little reorganization and rewriting, you can focus on making the minor changes. After rewriting, you may want to repeat the review step.

2. Proofreading—After review and rewriting, you should produce a final draft as perfect as you can make it. When you have your final draft, you will need to proofread it. Proofreading involves looking very closely at all the details of your writing to make sure that there are no accidental or overlooked errors. Spelling and punctuation are some of the details to consider. Make any corrections necessary.

C. Sharing/Publishing

Once you have proofread and corrected any errors, you are ready to share your writing with its intended audience or publish it for wider distribution.

Evaluation

As you review, revise, proofread, and publish your writing, keep in mind that your essay will be evaluated on:

Ideas and Information—Is it detailed and specific enough to help the reader?
Organization—Does your first paragraph introduce the idea, your middle paragraphs explain it, and your last paragraph review the idea?
Sentence Structure—Do you have complete sentences with correct verb tenses?
Word Use—Do you use content words appropriately?
Punctuation Plus—Are your paragraphs indented? Do you have capital letters at the beginning of sentences and full stops at the end?

7.5 Extend

Beyond the Classroom—The United States has 56 national parks, 72 national monuments, 211 national historic parks, and 54 national recreation areas, seashores, and trails. Each state also has its own state parks, monuments, historic sites, and recreation areas. Find out more about one of these areas near you. Visit one. While there, carefully observe your surroundings, using all of your senses. Write a paragraph to describe a particularly memorable aspect of the site.

Using Technology—On the Internet, there are now a number of open-content Web sites that encourage writers to contribute their knowledge to the site. These sites collect and organize this information so that people can have an extensive, up-to-date resource. Wikipedia <en.wikipedia.org> offers an online open-content encyclopedia and other resources. Wikitravel <www.wikitravel.org> and World 66 <www.world66.com> are open-content travel guides. Explore each of these sites. Look for information about your hometown and country. Use your description essay as a resource and contribute some information to one of the sites. You will be a published writer.

Chapter 8—Comparison and Contrast

This chapter builds on the previous chapter about descriptive writing. It incorporates descriptions into the process of comparing and contrasting two things.

8.1 Engage—Debating a Social Issue

This activity gives you the opportunity to debate a social issue.

Throughout history, women have been involved in fighting wars. These historical women not only supported the fighting men and served as nurses, they also fought as warriors alongside the men, and often led men into battle. Almost every culture has its stories of women warriors—Queen Vishpla of India, Queen Ahotep I of Egypt, Zabibi and Samsi of Arabia, Trung Trac and Trung Nhi of Vietnam, Himoko of Japan, Fa Mulan of China, Queen Mavia of the Bedouins, the Amazons of Greek legend, and Joan of Arc of France—to name a few. However, although their women have often proven their courage and strength on the battlefield, most cultures have had restrictions against women in combat. In modern times, as women have won more and more rights, countries have faced heated debates about whether or not women should be allowed in combat. In the United States, women were allowed to serve in the Navy on combat ships and in the Air Force on fighter planes, beginning in 1994. The Army and Marines have opened up more and more occupations and positions to women, putting women closer to the front lines.

Each time women gain more rights and take on more challenges, the country fights a battle of opinions and public policy.

Your Dilemma—Should women be allowed to fight in combat?

Imagine that you are senators in the U.S. Senate. You must decide: Women in combat? Why or why not?

Forming Groups: Divide the students into "debate groups" of four to six. Within these groups, assign half of the students the For argument and half the Against argument.

1. Based on the argument assigned to you by your professor, read and prepare a case for one of the sides described below.

> **For:** You must argue that women SHOULD be allowed to fight in combat. Develop with your partners strong reasons why women should serve in all positions in the military, including dangerous ones such as combat. What are the characteristics of women that would allow them to participate in activities traditionally limited to men?

> **Against:** You must argue that women SHOULD NOT be allowed to fight in combat. With your partners, develop strong reasons why women should not serve in all positions

in the military, especially dangerous ones such as combat. What are the characteristics of women that would be barriers to their participation in activities traditionally limited to men?

2. With your partners, take 10 minutes to develop a case with strong reasons. Find another group with the same assignment (a shared interest group). Work together for 10 minutes to exchange ideas and strengthen each other's arguments. (Use a total of 20 minutes.)

3. Return to your original debate group. The group with the For argument should present first, taking five minutes to make its case with the evidence (firm and soft) that the group members find most persuasive. The Against group should be silent during this presentation phase. Then, the group with the Against argument should present, also taking five minutes to make its case with the evidence (firm and soft) that its members find most persuasive. Again, the For group should be silent during this presentation phase. When both groups have finished their presentations, they can debate back and forth for five minutes. (Use a total of 15 minutes.)

4. Together as an entire class, have a representative from your group summarize the main arguments from your presentation. The other groups will do the same. Conduct a vote to gauge the personal views of each individual student. (Use 10 minutes)

5. Write a paragraph for homework summarizing your views.

8.2 Explore—Similarities and Differences

Nouns can be described by their similarities and differences. They generally have some characteristics that are similar and some that are different. The degree to which they are similar or different depends on the amount or importance of their similarities compared to their differences. Two things that have all characteristics that are the same are called identical.

This activity is a follow up to your discussion of men and women. Either by yourself or in groups with your classmates, list the characteristics of men, women, and both genders. (Table 8.1 gives an example of how to organize your lists.) Try to include as many characteristics as you can think of and put them in the appropriate column.

Table 8.1—Comparison of Men and Women

Men	Both	Women

Examine the types of characteristics that you have listed. Try to find three or four categories (classifications) that all of your characteristics can fit under. List those categories here.

Category 1—

Category 2—

Category 3—

Category 4—

8.3 Explain—Compare and Contrast Essay

The compare and contrast essay allows a writer to explore the similarities and/or the differences between two (sometimes more) people, places, things, or concepts. This type of writing is essentially description, but it is a description of two (or more) things in order to highlight characteristics they have in common and/or characteristics that they do not share.

Compare and contrast relationships can be very complicated, with numerous similarities and differences. Some of these similarities and differences are obvious and trivial (of little importance). Others are more interesting and more important. The purpose of the essay and its audience will help determine which similarities and differences are interesting. The thesis should include focusing tools that target the interesting and important characteristics.

The thesis for a compare and contrast essay often includes a focus on similarities OR a focus on differences. When it is necessary or useful to describe both the similarities and differences, a writer usually creates one section of the body for similarities and another section of the body for differences.

Organizing Similarities and Differences

When writers arrange their descriptions of similarities and/or differences, they commonly use one of the following methods of organization—point-by-point, block-by-block, or a combination of the two.

Point-by-point—With point-by-point organization, the writer first describes one of the highlighted characteristics of the first subject and then follows this with a description of the same highlighted characteristic of the second subject. For example, if you were comparing your brother and sister, you might first describe your brother's hair and then your sister's hair. Then, you might describe your brother's facial features and then your sister's facial features. You would continue back and forth for each highlighted characteristic.

Point-by-point organization is like a tennis match. The ball goes back and forth from one player to the other, back and forth, back and forth, until the points are finished. This type of organization is useful when trying to emphasize how the individual parts are related. But, just as a tennis match can become monotonous to the spectator—the ball going back and forth, back and forth, back and forth, over and over—if point-by-point organization continues for too long without a break, the reader will grow tired of the back and forth.

Block-by-block—With block-by-block organization, the writer first describes all of the highlighted characteristics of the first subject and then follows this with a description of all of the highlighted characteristics of the second subject. If the comparison is complex, the writer may create a block of descriptions for one set of related characteristics for the first subject and then the second; then, the writer does a second block of descriptions for a second set of related characteristics for each subject, and so on. To return to our example, if you were comparing your brother and sister, you would first describe all of the physical characteristics of your brother and then you would describe all of the physical characteristics of your sister.

Block-by-block organization is more like an American football game. One team gets the ball and holds onto it until it scores or it cannot advance. Then, the other team gets the ball and holds onto it until it scores or it cannot advance. Block-by-block organization is useful when trying to show how whole things are related. It does not cause readers to grow tired of the back-and-forth comparisons. However, because individual characteristics do not appear side by side, the writer will often need to make connections between characteristics to remind the reader of points already made.

Related Structures

Comparatives

Adjectives are used to describe or give more information about a noun. Adjectives can also be used to compare two nouns using the same characteristic. These are **comparatives**.

Forming the comparative:

Focus on similarities

... as (adjective) as ...

Focus on differences

... (adjective) +-er than ... OR ... more (adjective) than ...
... less (adjective) than ...
... not as (adjective) as ...

If the regular form of an adjective has one syllable, or two syllables AND ends with a *-y* (not *-ly*) or *-le*, you can make the comparative by adding *-er* (change the final *-y* to an *i*). If the regular form has two or more syllables, you should use *more* to make the comparative. Some adjectives such as bad and good have irregular comparatives.

Examples:

Regular form	Comparative
amazing	more (less) amazing than
ancient	more (less) ancient than
bad	worse than
beautiful	more (less) beautiful than
big	bigger than
boring	more (less) boring than
delicious	more (less) delicious than
disgusting	more (less) disgusting than
futuristic	more (less) futuristic than
good	better than
immense	more (less) immense than
new	newer than
old	older than
simple	simpler than
tiny	tinier than
ugly	uglier than
wide	wider than

Example sentences:

American cuisine is delicious.
French cuisine is more delicious than American cuisine.

The Sears Tower in Chicago is tall.
The Petronas Towers in Kuala Lumpur are taller than the Sears Tower.

A brook is not very wide.
A creek is wider than a brook.

Shortened and Reduced Adjective Clauses

In Chapter 7, you explored the use of adjective clauses as a way of putting more description in writing. Experienced writers of English use adjective clauses to make their writing more descriptive, but they often shorten the clauses to eliminate the wordiness of their sentences. This may mean deleting one word (often the clause marker) or reducing the clause (by deleting the clause subject and the clause verb) to make the clause into a phrase.

Deleting the Clause Marker—In many cases, when the clause marker serves as the object of the clause, it can be deleted without loss of clear meaning. Some examples:

The painter <u>whom we met at Frank's party</u> is having a special exhibition of his works at Gallery Five.
The painter <u>we met at Frank's party</u> is having a special exhibition of his works at Gallery Five.

The home team won the basketball game <u>that we watched on television at the sports bar</u>.
The home team won the basketball game <u>we watched on television at the sports bar</u>.

Tourism in Georgia increased during the summer <u>when the Olympic Games were held in Atlanta</u>.
Because you could also write this sentence as: "Tourism in Georgia increased during the summer <u>that the Olympic Games were held in Atlanta</u>," you can delete the clause marker.
Tourism in Georgia increased during the summer <u>the Olympic Games were held in Atlanta</u>.

Creating Appositives—One way to reduce adjective clauses into phrases is to create **appositives**. Appositives are nouns, noun phrases, or noun substitutes that come immediately after a noun to give more information about that noun. Appositives are usually set off from the main clause of the sentence by commas. Typically, if the adjective clause uses the clause marker as the clause subject and uses BE as the clause verb, it can be reduced to an appositive by deleting the clause subject and clause verb. Some examples:

The author <u>who was one of the first writers to write detective stories</u> influenced many twentieth-century American mystery writers.
The author, <u>one of the first writers to write detective stories</u>, influenced many twentieth-century American mystery writers.

Dr. Hobart James will replace the outgoing president, <u>who was Gerald Dahl</u>, on the planning council.
Dr. Hobart James will replace the outgoing president, <u>Gerald Dahl</u>, on the planning council.

The team hoped one day to return to their favorite climbing sites, <u>which were Mt. Kilimanjaro and Mt. Fuji</u>.
The team hoped one day to return to their favorite climbing sites, <u>Mt. Kilimanjaro and Mt. Fuji</u>.

Reducing Adjective Clauses to Adjective Phrases—If an adjective clause uses the clause marker as its subject and a form of the verb BE as the clause verb, it can also be reduced to an adjective phrase. This reduction is available if BE is part of a progressive verb (BE plus a verb in present participle form [-ing]) or a passive verb (BE plus a verb in past participle form [-ed, -en, irregular]). It is also available if BE is followed by an adjective linked to a prepositional phrase or by a comparative adjective phrase. Some examples:

The people <u>who are moving into the house next door</u> have five dogs, sixteen cats, and a large snake.
The people <u>moving into the house next door</u> have five dogs, sixteen cats, and a large snake.

The movie <u>that was filmed on location in my home country</u> won the Academy Award for best foreign language picture.
The movie <u>filmed on location in my home country</u> won the Academy Award for best foreign language picture.

The agency has been reorganized. <u>The agency is responsible for issuing permission to study in the United States</u>.
The agency <u>that is responsible for issuing permission to study in the United States</u> has been reorganized.
The agency <u>responsible for issuing permission to study in the United States</u> has been reorganized.

Archeologists have found South American civilizations. <u>These civilizations were more advanced than European civilizations of the same historical period</u>.
Archeologists have found South American civilizations <u>that were more advanced than European civilizations of the same historical period</u>.
Archeologists have found South American civilizations <u>more advanced than European civilizations of the same historical period</u>.

If writers can rewrite one of the sentences to be combined into a clause that uses BE as the clause verb, they can then reduce the clause into a phrase. This is possible for the purpose of making a reduced adjective clause even with stative verbs, which normally do not allow progressive forms. Some examples:

That man is a famous actor. <u>He is at the table in the corner</u>.
That man is a famous actor. <u>He is sitting at the table in the corner</u>.
That man <u>who is sitting at the table in the corner</u> is a famous actor.
That man <u>sitting at the table in the corner</u> is a famous actor.

At the fund raiser, we sold the pumpkin pies. <u>My mother baked the pumpkin pies</u>.
At the fund raiser, we sold the pumpkin pies. <u>The pumpkin pies were baked by my mother</u>.
At the fund raiser, we sold the pumpkin pies <u>that were baked by my mother</u>.
At the fund raiser, we sold the pumpkin pies <u>baked by my mother</u>.

Anyone is asked to call the local police. <u>That person knows the whereabouts of Arthur Johnson</u>.
Anyone <u>who knows the whereabouts of Arthur Johnson</u> is asked to call the local police.
Anyone <u>who (is knowing) the whereabouts of Arthur Johnson</u> is asked to call the local police. (*Is knowing* is not permitted in sentences and clauses because *know* is a stative verb. It is permitted here as an interim step useful in understanding how the clause is reduced to a phrase.)
Anyone <u>knowing the whereabouts of Arthur Johnson</u> is asked to call the local police.

Reducing Adjective Clauses to Prepositional Phrases—If an adjective clause uses the clause marker as the clause subject and the verb BE as the clause verb, it can also be reduced to a prepositional phrase if such a phrase immediately follows the BE verb. Some examples:

The fountain was designed by a world-renowned artist. <u>The fountain is in the courtyard of the student union</u>.
The fountain <u>that is in the courtyard of the student union</u> was designed by a world-renowned artist.
The fountain <u>in the courtyard of the student union</u> was designed by a world-renowned artist.

The performance features the National Ballet Company of Thailand. <u>The performance is at the Kennedy Center</u>.
The performance <u>that is at the Kennedy Center</u> features the National Ballet Company of Thailand.
The performance <u>at the Kennedy Center</u> features the National Ballet Company of Thailand.

The doctor will give a lecture in the last week of the semester. <u>The doctor is from the newest department at the medical school</u>.
The doctor <u>who is from the newest department at the medical school</u> will give a lecture in the last week of the semester.
The doctor <u>from the newest department at the medical school</u> will give a lecture in the last week of the semester.

Misplaced Modifiers

In this and the previous chapters, you have reviewed words, phrases, and clauses used to modify (describe or give more information about) nouns. In English, adjectives typically precede the nouns that they modify. Adjective clauses, adjective phrases (reduced clauses), and prepositional phrases often immediately follow the nouns that they modify. These modifiers can also come immediately before the nouns that they modify.

In trying to be descriptive, especially when combining sentences, writers sometimes put modifiers in the wrong place. The modifiers may be separated from the nouns that they modify. If there are other nouns in the sentence, there may be confusion as to which noun is being modified. Or, there may be confusion because the noun being modified is completely absent from the sentence. This confusion may cause serious or humorous misunderstandings.

In the movie "Mary Poppins," Mary's uncle shows how misplaced modifiers can be funny:

First person: "I know a man with a wooden leg named Smith."
Second person: "What is the name of his other leg?"

The source of the humorous misunderstanding is that the modifier *named Smith* comes immediately after the noun *leg*. So, because the rule is that phrases and clauses modify the noun that they follow, according to this sentence, the man's leg is named Smith. In reality, the man (not his leg) is named Smith. The sentence should read:

"I know a man named Smith with a wooden leg." The man is named Smith and Smith has a wooden leg.

Other examples:

Dancers performed a humorous piece for the politicians dressed as clowns.
The dancers, not the politicians, were dressed as clowns. So, the sentence should read:
Dancers dressed as clowns performed a humorous piece for the politicians.

Along the downtown streets, merchants have placed holiday banners.
The banners, not the merchants, are along the downtown streets. So, the sentence should read:
Merchants have placed holiday banners along the downtown streets.

Even though they smelled rotten, the chefs served the bananas.
The bananas, not the chefs, smelled rotten. So, the sentence should read:
The chefs served the bananas even though they smelled rotten.

Hoping to impress consumers interested in safety, air bags have been placed in front and rear seats.
This sentence suggests that air bags are hoping to impress, but air bags do not hope. This sentence actually lacks the noun modified by the adjective phrase. To correct the sentence, a writer would have to add the appropriate noun in the correct place. For example,
Hoping to impress consumers interested in safety, the Jupiter Corporation has placed air bags in front and rear seats.

How can a writer correct misplaced modifiers and eliminate misunderstandings?

1. Move the modifier to the appropriate place immediately after the noun it modifies;
2. If the noun is missing, add the noun in the appropriate place;
3. Or, in some cases, a writer may need to break a long, combined sentence into two or more sentences to make the complex ideas clear.

8.4 Exercise / Evaluate

Exercise 1: Warm-up Writing

In a paragraph (10-12 sentences), compare and contrast your parents (or two other people in your family). Use details and descriptive language. You may want to compare their physical characteristics, their personalities, their behavior, their roles in the family, their roles beyond the family, or a combination of these.

Exercise 2:　Related Structure/Skills

A.　Comparatives—Write two sentences for each of the following adjectives.　Use the regular form in the first sentence and the comparative form in the second sentence.

Example:　　Gaston was very pleased that he had climbed the <u>high</u> mountain near his home. He was quite jealous when his brother climbed a <u>higher</u> mountain.

1. admirable
2. angry
3. complex
4. credible
5. definite
6. diverse
7. evident
8. fast
9. feasible
10. heavy
11. hot
12. little
13. precise
14. rigid
15. trivial

B.　Misplaced Modifiers—Rewrite the following sentences to correct the misunderstandings caused by misplaced modifiers.

Example:　　I know a man with a wooden leg named Smith. I know a man named Smith with a wooden leg.

1. I met the conductor who started the local orchestra from Germany.
2. The widow was reluctant to talk about the death of her husband in a press conference with several journalists.
3. Climbing a tree, the sunset was more beautiful.
4. Even though some are very strange, the ESL teachers agreed to let the students demonstrate their customs.
5. The city council voted to make it illegal for women to sell hot dogs dressed in skimpy bikinis.
6. Blackened and looking like a giant raisin, my aunt still served the Thanksgiving turkey.
7. At the basketball game, an announcement was made that the wallet belonging to a spectator that I had found at one of the concession stands was being held at the box office.
8. We saw many exotic animals walking around at the zoo.
9. The pop singer sang a special song for the president wearing a dress that left very little to the imagination.
10. The young fourteen-year-old boy signed a contract to play professional soccer on the steps of the Lincoln Memorial in Washington, D.C.

Exercise 3: Focused Writing Practice

Comparative paragraph cloze. Read the following excerpt from an essay by the American writer Mark Twain (1835-1910). After you have read the excerpt, fill each blank with a word that fits the grammar and the meaning of the words around it.

There are several kinds of stories, but only one difficult kind—the humorous. I will talk mainly about that one. The humorous story is American; _____ comic story is English; the witty story is French. The _____ story depends for its effect upon the manner _____ the telling; the comic story and the witty story upon _____ matter [content].

The humorous story may be spun out to great length. _____ may wander around as much as it pleases, and arrive nowhere _____ particular; but the comic and witty stories must be brief _____ end with a point. The humorous story bubbles gently _____; the others burst.

The humorous story is strictly a work _____ art—high and delicate art—and only an artist can _____ it; but no art is necessary in telling the comic story_____ the witty story. Anybody can do it. The art of _____ a humorous story—understand, I mean by word of mouth, _____ print—was created in America, and has remained at home.

_____ humorous story is told gravely. The teller does his best _____ conceal the fact that he even dimly suspects that there _____ anything funny about it; but the teller of the comic _____ tells you beforehand that it is one of the funniest _____ he has ever heard, then tells it with eager delight. _____ is [then] the first person to laugh when he gets through. _____ sometimes, if he has had good success, he is _____ glad and happy that he will repeat the "nub" of _____ and glance around from face to face, collecting applause, _____ then repeat it again. It is a pathetic thing to see.

From "How to Tell a Story," by Mark Twain, in *How to Tell a Story and Others,* 1897.

In your favorite search engine, search for this essay by typing in the title and author. Read the entire essay. Then, check the exercise above against the original to compare your answers.

Exercise 4: Compare and Contrast Essay Assignment

This assignment will give you practice writing a compare and contrast essay. In comparing and contrasting, you will have the opportunity to describe the similarities and/or the differences between people, places, things, or concepts. Because compare and contrast essays are a type of description, you need to continue to use vivid details in your writing. This type of writing is important. People find it useful to establish the similarities or differences between things; the things compared can be seen or treated or valued similarly or differently, as appropriate. Compare and contrast essays usually focus on current observations and, therefore, use present tense verbs. If the comparison chooses subjects from the past or future, it would use past tense verbs or future tense verbs as needed. Compare and contrast essays most often use third person nouns and pronouns (he, she, it, they) as grammatical subjects.

Comparing and Contrasting Men and Women. Decide on the basis of your discussions and gathering of ideas in the "Engage" and "Explore" activities above which of the following thesis statements you believe is most accurate.

Men and women are basically the same. OR, Men and women are fundamentally different.

Using the thesis statement that you have chosen, the information you gathered above, and other evidence you can gather, write a five-to-seven-paragraph essay to describe in detail the most important characteristics that make men and women similar, OR the most significant characteristics that make men and women different. Your audience is people who make policy decisions concerning the opportunities of men and women in education, in the workplace, and in other areas of society. Your purpose is to provide these people with information useful to them in making their decisions.

Using the Writing Process

Follow the steps of the writing process spelled out below to help complete your essay.

I. Before Writing

A. Getting Ideas—Focused Free Writing

The purpose of free writing is to get ideas by writing for a chosen length of time about anything that comes into your head without stopping to worry about grammar, punctuation, or spelling. Focused free writing requires you to write whatever comes into your head about a specific topic that you or someone else has chosen.

Write down, in sentences, everything that comes to mind about your topic. There are no bad ideas. Even silly or irrelevant ideas can be turned into good ideas with a little work. If you cannot think of anything, write the same word again and again. Now, on a separate sheet of paper, write for 10 minutes about:

The similarities and differences between men and women.

After the 10 minutes have passed, read your free writing and underline any information that might be useful in writing an essay about the thesis that you chose above:

Men and women are basically the same. OR, Men and women are fundamentally different.

You may discover after focused free writing that you need to change or add additional focusing tools to your thesis. You may find that you do not know enough about a topic to write about it, and you need more information. This is an advantage to free writing. You save time by quickly finding out in the early stages of writing that you need to make changes or gather more information.

B. Grouping Ideas

In the "Explore" activity above, you developed three or four categories for the characteristics that you listed. You can use those categories to organize your ideas here. When writers and researchers describe, compare, or contrast human beings, they often classify their information according to physical, psychological, and social/cultural characteristics. How do these categories compare to the ones you found? Decide which categories you would like to use and their order in your essay. Also, decide if you would prefer to use point-by-point OR block-by-block organization. Below are two outline models, one for point-by-point and one for block-by-block. Use the model that fits your approach and create an outline on a separate sheet of paper.

Point-by-Point

Women   Men

Category 1: _____

   a. _____   a. _____
   b. _____   b. _____
   c. _____   c. _____
   d. _____   d. _____

Category 2: _____

   a. _____   a. _____
   b. _____   b. _____
   c. _____   c. _____
   d. _____   d. _____

Category 3: _____

   a. _____   a. _____
   b. _____   b. _____
   c. _____   c. _____
   d. _____   d. _____

Category 4: _____

   a. _____   a. _____
   b. _____   b. _____
   c. _____   c. _____
   d. _____   d. _____

Block-by-Block

<u>Women</u>

Category 1: _____

   a. _____
   b. _____
   c. _____
   d. _____

Category 2: _____

   a. _____
   b. _____
   c. _____
   d. _____

Category 3: _____

   a. _____
   b. _____
   c. _____
   d. _____

Category 4: _____

   a. _____
   b. _____
   c. _____
   d. _____

<u>Men</u>

Category 1: _____

   a. _____
   b. _____
   c. _____
   d. _____

Category 2: _____

    a. _____
    b. _____
    c. _____
    d. _____

Category 3: _____

    a. _____
    b. _____
    c. _____
    d. _____

Category 4: _____

    a. _____
    b. _____
    c. _____
    d. _____

II. During Writing

A. Planning

<u>1. Establishing the Writing Context</u>

Write out the plan for your writing. Include the following information.

To whom? (Audience):
What? (Form) Decide if you will use point-by-point or block-by-block organization:
When and Where? (Setting):
Why? (Purpose):
How? (Process):
Which? (Sources):

<u>2. Formulating a Main Idea</u>

<u>3. Developing Support</u>

<u>4. Organizing</u>

(Use the Essay Template below for help in completing numbers 2, 3, and 4.)

Essay Template

Your name: _____   Audience: _____

Professor's name: _____   Purpose: _____

Course name: _____   Essay type: <u>Comparison</u>

Date: _____   Source: _____

Title: _____

Introduction

Invitation (complete sentence):

Orientation (notes; include information about why the intended audience would be interested in this general topic):

Thesis statement (complete sentence; include a clear indication that the essay is a comparison):

Body

First Subject to Be Compared (block-by-block) OR Group of Related Characteristics (set of point-by-point comparisons)—Topic sentence (complete sentence):

<u>Firm evidence (notes)</u>   <u>Soft evidence (notes)</u>

Second Subject to Be Compared (block-by-block) OR Group of Related Characteristics (set of point-by-point comparisons)—Topic sentence (complete sentence):

<u>Firm evidence (notes)</u>   <u>Soft evidence (notes)</u>

Other Subject to Be Compared (if needed) OR Group of Related Characteristics—Topic sentence (complete sentence):

Firm evidence (notes)   Soft evidence (notes)

Conclusion

Transition (word, phrase, or none):

Restatement of thesis statement (complete sentence):

Summary of main points (notes):

Final thought (complete sentence):

Initial Self-Review

Strengths of the essay:

Weaknesses of the essay:

Actions needed to address weaknesses:

II. *During Writing* (continued)

B. Writing

1. <u>Outside In.</u> By completing the essay template above, you have created a framework for your essay. You have the main ideas for the important parts of the essay. Now, all that you need to do is to add the supporting details in complete sentences. Use the essay template to guide your writing.

Read over your completed essay to assure that you have utilized the six elements of good paragraph and essay development—topic, focus, support, logic, unity, and coherence. (See Chapter 2 for a review of these elements.) For this essay, pay special attention to the logic of your arrangement. Did you use point-by-point, block-by-block, or a combination of both? Do your coherence techniques help make clear the characteristics that you are comparing? Make changes or additions to improve the organization.

III. *After Writing*

A. Reviewing

1. <u>Self-Review.</u> After you have written your compare and contrast essay, complete the following sheet, "Responding to a First Draft," to make sure that you have focused on the assignment and included all the appropriate elements of a good paper. Try to answer the questions in as much detail as you can. The purpose of the sheet is to help you focus on what you are doing and encourage you to take responsibility for your own work. Do your best to make the paper as effective as you can.

Responding to a First Draft

Answer the following questions with as much detail as you can. Answering these questions will require you to show that you understand what is being done in the paper.

General

1. What is the title? It should give an idea of the main idea of the paper.

2. Who is the main intended audience? Who should read this essay? Check one.
_____General readers   _____Specific groups   _____Experts
_____The writer's peers   _____One specific person   _____The writer her/himself

3. What is the main purpose? (check one)
_____Share or Express   _____Inform or Explain   _____Prove or Persuade

4. What form is used primarily? (check one)
___Narrative   ___Process   ___Classification and Division
___Description   ___Comparison and Contrast   ___Evaluation
___Cause and Effect   ___Problem and Solution

Introduction

5. Does the paper have an introductory paragraph? If not, how is the reader oriented to the information presented?

6. The Invitation. How is the reader's interest in this paper attracted? (check one)
___a funny story   ___a difficult question   ___a famous quotation
___a challenge   ___a similar or different experience   ___something new
___something old in a new light   ___a statement of general interest

7. What is the thesis statement? (main idea sentence)

8. How was the general topic focused? (Check all that apply.)
___time   ___place   ___number or sequence   ___category or characteristic
___similarity/difference   ___quality   ___cause/effect   ___problem/solution

Body

9. What are the three to five main points developed in the body of the paper?

10. Do they support the thesis statement? How?

11. Are there points that could be added or removed? What are they?

12. What forms of evidence have been used? (Check all that apply.)
___facts and statistics   ___observations   ___records   ___expert testimony
___precedents   ___analogies   ___experience   ___opinions

13. Is the evidence adequate to convince the readers? If not, what should be done?

Conclusion

14. Is there a concluding paragraph?   If not, how is the reader reminded of the key points?

15. Which of the following is included in the conclusion? (Check all that apply.)
_____a restatement of thesis   _____a summary of main points
_____a famous quotation related to thesis   _____a call to action

16. Does the paper give a feeling of completeness?   If not, what is missing, and what should be done?

Sentence Structure, Word Use, and Punctuation

17. Carefully check each of the following items to assure that as many mistakes as possible have been corrected.

___complete sentences   ___appropriate verb tenses   ___uses transitions
___subject/verb agreement   ___correct word forms   ___spelling
___correct word order   ___capitals and full stops   ___format
___modifiers correctly located

Plan for Second Draft

18. What questions need to be answered before the next draft? What changes need to be made?

III. After Writing (continued)

A. Reviewing

2. Peer Review. Share your completed essay with one of your classmates. Have her/him respond to your first draft by writing the following on a separate sheet of paper:

Peer Response

a. Write three things that you found interesting about your classmate's paper.

b. Write three questions that you have now that you have read your classmate's paper.

c. Write three suggestions that you have for your classmate to incorporate into her/his next draft.

3. Expert Review. Share your draft with a native speaker who is an experienced writer—a peer at your college, a tutor, a writing-center instructor, or your writing professor. Ask for specific feedback about questions and concerns that you have about your paper. Your final draft will be evaluated on the areas listed in the "Evaluation" section below, so be sure to identify the areas and specific points with which you need the most help.

B. Finishing

1. Rewriting

After you have feedback from you own review and the review of others, you need to rewrite your essay. If you have a lot of reorganization and rewriting to do, you will want to return to the writing step above and follow those guidelines again. If you have little reorganization and rewriting, you can focus on making the minor changes. After rewriting, you may want to repeat the review step.

2. Proofreading

After review and rewriting, you should produce a final draft as perfect as you can make it. When you have your final draft, you will need to proofread it. Proofreading involves looking very closely at all the details of your writing to make sure that there are no accidental or overlooked errors. Spelling and punctuation are some of the details to consider.

C. Sharing/Publishing

Once you have proofread and corrected any errors, you are ready to share your writing with its intended audience or publish it for wider distribution.

Evaluation

As you review, revise. proofread, and publish your writing, keep in mind that your essay will be evaluated on:

Ideas and Information—Is it detailed and specific enough to help the reader?

Organization—Does your first paragraph introduce the idea, your middle paragraphs explain it, and last paragraph review the idea?

Sentence Structure—Do you have complete sentences with correct verb tenses?

Word Use—Do you use content words appropriately?

Punctuation Plus—Are your paragraphs indented? Do you have capital letters at the beginning of sentences and full stops at the end?

8.5 Extend

Additional Ideas—Comparisons can be helpful when you are trying to explain something that is complicated or unfamiliar to your audience. You describe or define what something is by explaining what it is like (or less often, not like). In the "Explain" section above, point-by-point organization is clarified by comparing it to a tennis match and block-by-block organization is compared to an American football game. These types of comparisons used to help explain something are called **analogies**.

With analogies, writers take a thing or concept that is known and understood and compare it to a thing or concept that is harder to understand. A good analogy will make a clear connection and help the reader understand easily. A bad analogy will fail to help the reader understand. One reason an analogy might fail is because the reader does not know and understand the analogy. For example, if you know nothing about American football, that analogy will not help you to understand the comparison to block-by-block organization.

Other types of comparisons that can be used to help explain something include **similes** and **metaphors**. Libraries often have reference books on analogies, similes, and metaphors. Ask your librarians for help finding information about these writing tools and share what you find with your classmates.

Writing tools such as analogies, similes, and metaphors can help to make your writing come alive for your readers, creating vivid images and connecting with their experiences. However, you need to be careful not to overuse these tools, or choose examples that are silly, confusing, or bad in other ways. You also need to be careful not to offer a **false analogy**, which, because the comparison has more differences than similarities, does not paint a true picture for the reader.

Literature—Because analogies, similes, and metaphors have such creative power, poets, novelists, and playwrights often use them. Here is the beginning of a poem by William Shakespeare (1564-1616), the English playwright and poet.

Sonnet XVIII

Shall I compare thee to a summer's day?
Thou art more lovely and more temperate...

Shakespeare goes on to compare the lady to the day. Skim through a book of poetry and note the analogies, similes, and metaphors used by the poets. Would the examples that you found be appropriate in an essay you are writing for one of your college courses? Why or why not?

Thinking Skills—A number of standardized tests use analogies to help judge a student's aptitude, or chance of success in undergraduate or graduate programs. These tests usually give the student a pair of words that have a certain relationship. Then, they give the student another word followed by several choices. The goal is to choose the word that creates the same relationship between the second set of words as with the first.

For example:

Tall is to Height as Wide is to _____. (The answer would be *Width*.)
Centimeter is to Inch as Kilogram is to _____. (The answer would be *Pound*.)

Try your skill at these analogy tests. You can find analogy tests in a bookstore, in test preparation guides. Or, you can search online for "analogy tests." Some sites offer free sample tests that allow people to practice.

Chapter 9—Evaluation

This chapter brings together the skills practiced in writing descriptions and comparisons from the previous two chapters and puts them to use in writing an evaluation essay.

9.1 Engage—Choose a World Language

This activity requires evaluating several alternatives and making the best choice.

With international travel more common and with the Internet making communication with all corners of the globe fast and easy, the world needs a universal or common language more than ever. The United Nations (UN), businesses, universities, and other organizations spend much time and money translating from one language to another. Some of these organizations have tried to simplify the problem by using official languages (the UN uses six official languages—Arabic, Chinese, English, French, Russian, and Spanish). Others have created new languages such as Esperanto or Volapuk to provide for universal communication, but few speak these constructed languages.

You have been asked to serve on an international task force to recommend a new *lingua franca*, or common language of international exchange.

1. Develop criteria (or standards) for choosing the best common language. In groups of three or four, make a list of the characteristics that a universal language should have. (Use about 10 minutes.)

2. List the alternatives. What are some languages that fit the criteria? Use your knowledge and experience to suggest choices. (Use about 5 minutes.)

3. Choose the language that you all agree is the best choice. Give some reasons why you think it is the best choice. (Use about 10 minutes.)

4. Outline the steps (the process) that countries would need to follow to help make your chosen language a universal language. Decide what needs to happen first, second, and so on. (Use about 15 minutes.)

5. Write a paragraph about your decision. Explain which language should become the world language, why, and how. (Use 15 to 20 minutes in class or as homework.)

9.2 Explore—Evaluating the Library

This activity has two parts. In the first part, you will practice setting standards. In the second part, you will do an analysis. You will use your analysis to complete an evaluation. The activity will also give you an opportunity to learn more about your library.

Part 1: Setting Standards—Your college is planning to build a new library. It wants this new library to be excellent, one of the best in the region. In order to include the ideas of students, the college has asked you for your input. What characteristics make a library excellent? (These are the standards for an excellent library.) What standards should an excellent library meet in the following areas?

In groups of three or four, establish standards for each of the areas below. In setting standards, be specific. You are trying to make a subjective term— "excellent" —objective by setting specific standards. You should (a) use numbers; (b) use specific examples; and (c) use specific descriptions. Make clear who, what, when, where, why, how much, and how many in appropriate areas. You may want to suggest numbers for the whole library or number per student enrolled.

What are the Characteristics of an Excellent Library?

A. Services
1. Access to materials
   Hours (days and times):

   Instructions for Using Material and Equipment (types and location):

   Equipment (hardware—types and numbers)
   - Computers:
   - Printers:
   - Computer peripherals:
   - Copy machines:
   - Audio players:
   - Video players:
   - Other hardware:

   Software
   - Types and availability:

2. Patron services
   Orientation and workshops:
   Borrowing privileges (what and how long):
   Assistance:
   Online services:
   Other services:

B. Physical facilities

Space
- Square footage:
- Study rooms:
- Study desks and tables:
- Other areas:

Bulletin boards or other information sources
- Number and location:
- Type of information:

Lighting
- Type:
- Location:

C. Atmosphere

Student behavior policies:
General ambiance and cleanliness:
Temperature:
Restrooms:
Food and drink access policies:

D. Staff

Number:
Knowledge and education requirements (degrees):
Behavior expectations (describe):

E. Collections

Scope
- General or specific (explain):
- Topics covered (examples):

Print materials (number and type)
- Number of actual items:
- Number of items indexed:
- Availability of materials:
- Timeliness (up to date?):
- Condition:

Other materials (number and type)
- Audio-visual materials:
- Electronic databases owned:
- Electronic resources accessible:

All of the groups should come together and the whole class should decide upon a list of standards for an excellent library, a list that includes standards for all of the areas above.

Part 2: Analysis—For this part, the class will go to the library. Divide the students in the class into four equal groups. Once at the library, each group will be responsible for gathering detailed information about the areas assigned to it. Each group can decide how best to divide the task. Sources for information include direct observation (measuring, counting, using the senses), asking questions of librarians and patrons, as well as consulting written information in brochures, handbooks, and other printed materials. After visiting the library itself, some groups may want to explore the library's Web site if available.

All students will need to gather clear and detailed information, because they will be sharing it with other members of their group and then with the entire class. The goal is to put together a detailed analysis that has information on all of the library's various areas.

Group 1

A. Services
1. Access to materials
      Hours (days and times):

      Instructions for Using Material and Equipment (types and location):

      Equipment (hardware—types and numbers)
- Computers:
- Printers:
- Computer peripherals:
- Copy machines:
- Audio players:
- Video players:
- Other hardware:

      Software
- Types and availability:

Group 2

2. Patron services
      Orientation and workshops:
      Borrowing privileges (what and how long):
      Assistance:
      Online services:
      Other services:

B. Physical facilities

Space
- Square footage:
- Study rooms:
- Study desks and tables:
- Other areas:

Bulletin boards or other information sources
- Number and location:
- Type of information:

Group 3

Lighting
- Type:
- Location:

C. Atmosphere

Student behavior policies:
General ambiance and cleanliness:
Temperature:
Restrooms:
Food and drink access policies:

D. Staff

Number:
Knowledge and education requirements (degrees):
Behavior expectations (describe):

Group 4

E. Collections

Scope
- General or specific (explain):
- Topics covered (examples):

Print materials (number and type)
- Number of actual items:
- Number of items indexed:
- Availability of materials:
- Timeliness (up to date?):
- Condition:

Other materials (number and type)
- Audio-visual materials:
- Electronic databases owned:
- Electronic resources accessible:

After the trip to the library, each group can share its information with the whole class. Another alternative is to form new groups with at least one member from each of the analysis groups. Each member of these new collection groups can then share information with the other students. The goal is to allow each student to fill in the entire analysis sheet, either with direct observation or through collection from classmates.

9.3 Explain—Evaluation Essay

People are evaluators. We want to know if things are good or bad. We are interested in good food, good clothing, good shelter, good friends, good entertainment, good schools, and good times. We want to know the best and the worst, and why. Before we spend our time, our energy, or our money, we want to know that something is worth it. So, we turn to evaluations. We ask friends and acquaintances. We read reviews. We consult rating organizations and agencies. Sometimes, we conduct our own evaluation.

Evaluations can be shared informally by word of mouth or brief written reviews. In a formal written evaluation essay, writers not only share an assessment of something (whether it is good or bad, the best or the worst), they also share the process they used to reach the judgment. This judgment, if built on firm evidence presented in a logical process, will be more convincing to readers. Keep in mind that if you know and trust people, you are more likely to accept their evaluations. However, if you don't know them and have no experience with their judgment, you will need them to earn your acceptance with firm evidence presented in a logical process.

The formal process of evaluation requires three basic steps:

Setting Standards—First, the writer needs to explain what is meant by good, bad, best, worst, or whatever evaluation is being made. This step is called setting standards or establishing criteria. If you are trying to decide if your college is a good college, you need first to describe the characteristics of a good college. In order to do this, you may consult experts and other reliable judges—sources of firm evidence. You may also use logic and firm evidence to support your own view.

Analyzing the Subject—Second, the writer analyzes the subject, observing and describing the same characteristics covered in the standards step. If the standards for a good college include success at placing graduates in jobs, then you should determine the success of your college at placing graduates in jobs.

Evaluating the Subject against the Standards—Third, the writer needs to compare the subject to the standards. If the subject is very similar to the standards, it earns the same value as the standards. If the subject is very different from the standards, it earns the opposite value. If your college shares most of the characteristics of a good college, it can be considered a good college. If not, it cannot.

Evaluation essays are related to description and comparison essays. The writer first describes the standards to be used in evaluation. Then, the writer compares the subject or subjects to the standards. When the standards and subjects are similar, they have the same value. When they are different, they have different values.

Related Structures

Evaluation Words

In the chapter on description, you learned that one category of adjectives is related to evaluation. There are numerous adjectives that can be used for evaluation. Here is a short list of adjectives that can be used to evaluate the quality of an item such as a film. The adjectives are arranged with the more positive term on the left and the more negative term on the right. (For a list of more of these adjectives, see "Evaluation Adjectives" in the "Extra" section at the end of the book.)

Positive	Negative
appealing	terrible
complete	deficient
delightful	unpleasant
enjoyable	offensive
excellent	poor
exceptional	typical
fine	coarse
good	bad
great	poor
important	minor
interesting	boring
major	minor
outstanding	mediocre
perfect	fallible
remarkable	commonplace
special	ordinary
splendid	plain
striking	unimpressive
strong	weak
successful	incapable
superior	inferior
thorough	limited
tremendous	minute
valuable	worthless
wonderful	dreadful

Superlatives

In previous chapters, you worked with adjectives used to describe and to compare two nouns. When an adjective is used to compare a noun with all others according to a shared characteristic, it is in the superlative form.

Forming the superlative:

... (the adjective) + -est ...

OR

... the most (adjective)...

... the least [adjective] ...

Superlatives follow the same guidelines as comparatives: If the regular form of the adjective has one syllable, or two syllables AND ends with a -*y* (not -*ly*) or -*le*, you can make the superlative by adding -*est* (change the final -*y* to an *i*). If the regular form has two or more syllables, you should use *most* to make the superlative. Some adjectives such as bad and good have irregular superlatives.

Examples:

Regular Form	Superlative
amazing	the most (least) amazing
ancient	the most (least) ancient
bad	the worst
beautiful	the most (least) beautiful
big	the biggest
boring	the most (least) boring
delicious	the most (least) delicious
disgusting	the most (least) disgusting
futuristic	the most (least) futuristic
good	the best
immense	the most (least) immense
new	the newest
old	the oldest
simple	the simplest
tiny	the tiniest
ugly	the ugliest
wide	the widest

Example sentences:

American cuisine is delicious.
My country's cuisine is the most delicious in the world.

The Sears Tower in Chicago is tall.
The Taipei 101 Tower in Taiwan is the tallest building in the world.

A brook is not very wide.
The Amazon River is the widest in the world.

Modal Auxiliaries and Related Forms

In setting the standards for an evaluation, it is important to establish which criteria are required, which are strongly advised, and which are preferred. Certain modal auxiliaries are useful in clarifying these standards. Here are some examples.

Requirement

must—An excellent library <u>must</u> be in an easily accessible location.
must not—An excellent library <u>must not</u> charge a fee to borrow a book.

Strong Advice

should—An excellent library <u>should</u> be open at least sixteen hours per day.
should not—An excellent library <u>should not</u> permit patrons to be loud and unruly.
ought to—An excellent library <u>ought to</u> provide study rooms for students to work together.

Preference

would rather—Students <u>would rather</u> study in a library with a lot of natural light.
It would be better if—<u>It would be better if</u> the library offered students a place to eat and drink while studying.

9.4 Exercise / Evaluate

Exercise 1: Warm-up Writing

In a paragraph (10-12 sentences), write a review of a movie, book, CD, performance, exhibit, restaurant, or form of entertainment that you have recently experienced. Be sure to describe it in enough detail so that your classmates and professor will have an adequate sense of your experience. Then, explain why it was good or bad, excellent or poor, or whatever term you chose. Consider using some of the evaluation adjectives offered above.

Exercise 2: Related Structure / Skills

Prioritizing—For each of the groups below, use your knowledge and experience to give the three most important criteria to use in evaluating that item. Number 1 should be most important; number 2 the second most important; and number 3 the third most important. For example, for a student choosing a college, the three most important criteria, in order, might be: (1) tuition cost; (2) programs; and (3) location.

Give the three most important evaluation criteria for:

A New Car
for a college student:
1.
2.
3.

for a family with small children:
1.
2.
3.

for a businessman who travels a lot:
1.
2.
3.

A Popular Film
in the action genre:
1.
2.
3.

in the romance genre:
1.
2.
3.

in the comedy genre:
1.
2.
3.

<u>A Vacation Spot</u>
for a group of college students:
1.
2.
3.

for a family with teenagers
1.
2.
3.

a group of grandparents:
1.
2.
3.

<u>A Computer System</u>
for a college student:
1.
2.
3.

for a large manufacturing company:
1.
2.
3.

for an elementary (primary) school:
1.
2.
3.

Exercise 3: Focused Writing Practice

Modal Auxiliaries—Choose one set of priorities from each of the groups in Exercise 2 above and write a mini-paragraph of three sentences describing the priorities. Use *must*, *must not*, *should*, *should not*, *ought to*, and other expressions from "Related Structures" above to establish your priorities. Also, use transition words where appropriate. You should have four mini-paragraphs when finished.

Exercise 4: Evaluation Essay Assignment

This assignment will give you practice writing an evaluation essay.   This type of essay requires you to assert that your subject is good or bad (or some other value judgment) and prove it through a formal presentation of evidence. Evaluations are stronger than opinions because evaluations are based on evidence. Evaluation essays are very useful because people want to know what is best, worst, or other evaluator. They read reviews of consumer products, books, music, movies, and other things so that they can spend their money wisely. They write evaluations of products, services, employees, and resources in order to assure quality and improvement. Evaluation essays, like compare and contrast essays, usually focus on current observations and, therefore, use present tense verbs. In some cases past tense verbs or future tense verbs may be appropriate to the context. Evaluations most often use third person nouns and pronouns (he, she, it, they) as grammatical subjects.

Evaluating Your College Library. Using the standards that you set and comparing them to the analysis that you made, decide if your library is good or bad, excellent or poor, or use other appropriate evaluation terms. One of the following thesis statements or something similar may work for this essay. (Substitute the name of your college or library.)

The State College library is excellent because it meets most of the criteria for an excellent library.

OR

The State College library is inadequate because it fails to meet most of the criteria for an excellent library.

Using the thesis statement that you have chosen, the information you gathered above in the "Explore" section, and other evidence you can gather, write a five-to-seven-paragraph essay to evaluate your college library. Be sure to include sections for each of the three parts of an evaluation: (1) setting the standards; (2) analyzing the subject; and (3) evaluating the subject against the standards. Your audience includes the library staff and college administrators, who can use your evaluation to help make improvements where necessary; students already at the school, who can use the information to take better advantage of the library's resources; and students considering enrolling in the college, who may use the information in deciding whether or not to attend.

Using the Writing Process

Follow the steps of the writing process spelled out below to help complete your essay.

I. Before Writing

A. Getting Ideas—Primary Research

When you went to the library to gather information, you were getting ideas through research. If you have to write about something that is unfamiliar to you, research is a good way to get ideas. In this case, because you gathered the information directly from the source (you made direct observations; you counted the chairs; you talked to the librarians), you conducted **primary**

research. Primary research is important in evaluations; the evaluator needs first-hand (primary) knowledge of the subject.

Use the ideas that you discovered while analyzing the library to write your evaluation.

B. Grouping Ideas

By completing the outline in the "Explore" activity above, you grouped your ideas according to the categories given. Because there are a large number of categories in your outline, you should choose one or two related sections to focus on. Fill in details on these sections.

II. During Writing

A. Planning

1. Write out the context for your writing. Include the following information.

Audience: _____
Form: _____
Setting: _____
Purpose: _____
Process: _____
Source: _____

2. Formulating a Main Idea
3. Developing Support
4. Organizing
      a. Outlining

Complete the following sentence outline to help you complete 2, 3, and 4 above and prepare for writing.

Chapter 4 introduced outlining and gave examples of basic outlines. A basic outline uses words and phrases to organize the ideas used in writing. Meaning is the focus, not grammar. The essay templates in previous chapters provided practice writing basic outlines with complete sentences for key parts of the outline. (See the "Extra" section at the end of the book for an Evaluation Essay Template.)

Another type of outline is the sentence outline. In a sentence outline, a writer organizes the ideas for the writing and puts these ideas into complete sentences. Because complete sentences are used, the writer needs to give more attention to grammar and other structural concerns. Sentence outlines require more time during the planning part of the writing process, but they help reduce the amount of time required in writing and often in revising.

To practice using a sentence outline, answer the questions below. Be sure to write complete, grammatically correct sentences.

Sentence Outline

Your name: _____   Audience: _____

Professor's name: _____   Purpose: _____

Course name: _____   Essay type: _____

Date: _____   Source: _____

Title: _____

I. Introduction

A. Write your invitation here. Write a complete sentence.

What type of invitation did you choose? A quotation, a question, a surprising comment, a brief definition, a general statement of fact, an explanation of the topic's importance, an explanation of the topic's timeliness, an appeal to common experience, an anecdote—a brief story related to the topic.

B. What background information (history, news story, interesting fact, statistics, other), if any, should your reader have as orientation to the topic? Describe that information here in one sentence.

C. What is your thesis? Write a complete sentence here. Remember: (1) use focusing tools to clarify the topic of the essay; (2) make the topic of your essay the subject of your sentence; (3) be specific but not too specific; (4) include a preview of your subtopics in the order that you will develop them. (Your thesis should clearly state if your evaluation is positive or negative.)

II. Body

A. Setting the Standards. What are the standards that your subject should meet? How did you determine that these standards are appropriate? Summarize your ideas in one sentence.

B. Analysis. Describe your subject in each of the areas chosen for the evaluation.

1. Write a topic sentence for the first area of your evaluation here. Write a complete sentence. Use coherence techniques to link this subtopic to your thesis. (Which coherence technique did you use? Transition or Repetition)

a. What objective evidence will you use to develop this subtopic? Summarize in one complete sentence the facts, statistics, expert testimony, observations, and/or records that you will use.

b. What subjective evidence (if any) will you use to develop this subtopic? Summarize in one complete sentence the analogies, precedents, opinions, and/or experience that you will use.

2. Write a topic sentence for the second area of your evaluation here. Write a complete sentence. Use coherence techniques to link this subtopic to your thesis. (Which coherence technique did you use? Transition or Repetition)

a. What objective evidence will you use to develop this subtopic? Summarize in one complete sentence the facts, statistics, expert testimony, observations, and/or records that you will use.

b. What subjective evidence (if any) will you use to develop this subtopic? Summarize in one complete sentence the analogies, precedents, opinions, and/or experience that you will use.

3. Repeat 1 and 2 for additional areas of your evaluation, if needed.

C. Evaluation. What is your overall evaluation of your subject? Which standards were most significant in making your final decision? Summarize your findings in one sentence.

III. Conclusion

A. What kind of transition will you use to help the reader go from the body to the conclusion?

B. What has the reader learned about your topic? Restate your thesis in new words. Write one complete sentence here.

C. Write a summary of your subtopics in one complete sentence here.

D. Give your reader something to think about as s/he leaves your paper. Write a resolution or final thought here. Make it a complete sentence. What type of resolution will you use? (What type of resolution did you choose? A quotation, a question, a surprising comment, a brief definition, a general statement of fact, an explanation of the topic's importance, an explanation of the topic's timeliness, an appeal to common experience, an anecdote—a brief story related to the topic.)

II. *During Writing* (continued)

B. Writing

1. <u>One Step after Another.</u> In preparing to write this evaluation, you have been taking a step-by-step approach, from conducting research to organizing your information to outlining. Continue now with the remaining steps. Write the introduction, the body (standards, analysis, evaluation), and finally the conclusion.

Bringing It All Together

Read over your completed essay. You want to make sure that you have connected the standards, analysis, and evaluation by using appropriate coherence techniques. Again, make sure that your paragraphs are built with topic, focus, support, logic, unity, and coherence. Does the presentation of your evidence and evaluation provide a convincing argument to your audience? Will the audience agree with your evaluation, or at least seriously consider it? Make a strong case.

III. *After Writing*

A. Reviewing

1. <u>Self-Review.</u> Remember that your audience also evaluates your writing. In a college class, the professor evaluates student writing formally. In other contexts, readers evaluate writing more informally. In either case, writing that is evaluated positively by its audience will be more effective in achieving its purpose. Read your evaluation essay with the following questions in mind. If you cannot answer yes to each question, make the changes needed to improve your writing.

Ideas and Information—Is the information accurate, appropriate, and detailed?
Organization—Does the essay follow the introduction, body, and conclusion framework? Does it use the standards, analysis, and evaluation pattern effectively?
Sentence Structure—Do the sentences meet the requirements of good, complete sentences? Is the grammar correct?
Word Use—Do the words chosen have the appropriate meaning and form? Do they follow the standards of conventional usage?
Punctuation Plus—Is the format, style, and punctuation appropriate?

2. <u>Peer Review</u>—Exchange your evaluation essay with a classmate. Each of you will read the other's essay and then complete the "Responding to a First Draft" for that paper. Try to be as detailed as possible in answering the questions. Your feedback will help your classmate make improvements to her/his first draft.

Responding to a First Draft

Answer the following questions with as much detail as you can. Answering these questions will require you to show that you understand what is being done in the paper.

General

1. What is the title? It should give an idea of the main idea of the paper.

2. Who is the main intended audience? Who should read this essay? Check one.

_____General readers   _____Specific groups   _____Experts
_____The writer's peers   _____One specific person   _____The writer her/himself

3. What is the main purpose? (check one)

_____Share or Express   _____Inform or Explain   _____Prove or Persuade

4. What form is used primarily? (check one)

___Narrative   ___Process   ___Classification and Division
___Description   ___Comparison and Contrast   ___Evaluation
___Cause and Effect   ___Problem and Solution

Introduction

5. Does the paper have an introductory paragraph? If not, how is the reader oriented to the information presented?

6. The Invitation. How is the reader's interest in this paper attracted? (check one)

___a funny story   ___a difficult question   ___a famous quotation
___a challenge   ___a similar or different experience ___something new
___something old in a new light   ___a statement of general interest

7. What is the thesis statement? (main idea sentence)

8. How was the general topic focused? (Check all that apply.)

___time   ___place   ___number or sequence   ___category or characteristic
___similarity/difference   ___quality   ___cause/effect   ___problem/solution

Body

9. What are the three to five main points developed in the body of the paper?

10. Do they support the thesis statement? How?

11. Are there points that could be added or removed? What are they?

12. What forms of evidence have been used? (Check all that apply.)
___facts and statistics   ___observations   ___records   ___expert testimony
___precedents   ___analogies   ___experience   ___opinions

13. Is the evidence adequate to convince the readers? If not, what should be done?

Conclusion

14. Is there a concluding paragraph? If not, how is the reader reminded of the key points?

15. Which of the following is included in the conclusion? (Check all that apply.)
_____a restatement of thesis   _____a summary of main points
_____a famous quotation related to thesis   _____a call to action

16. Does the paper give a feeling of completeness? If not, what is missing, and what should be done?

Sentence Structure, Word Use, and Punctuation

17. Carefully check each of the following items to assure that as many mistakes as possible have been corrected.

___complete sentences   ___appropriate verb tenses   ___uses transitions
___subject/verb agreement   ___correct word forms   ___spelling
___correct word order   ___capitals and full stops   ___format
___modifiers correctly located

Plan for Second Draft

18. What questions need to be answered before the next draft? What changes need to be made?

III. After Writing (continued)

A. Reviewing

3. Expert Review. Share your draft with a native speaker who is an experienced writer—a peer at your school, a tutor, or a writing-center instructor. Ask for specific feedback about questions and concerns that you have about your paper. Your final draft will be evaluated on the areas mentioned above in the "Self-Review" step, so be sure to identify the areas and specific points with which you need the most help.

B. Finishing

1. Rewriting

After you have feedback from you own review and the review of others, you need to rewrite your essay. If you have a lot of reorganization and rewriting to do, you will want to return to the writing step above and follow those guidelines again. If you have little reorganization and rewriting, you can focus on making the minor changes. After rewriting, you may want to repeat the review step.

2. Proofreading

After reviewing and rewriting, you should produce a final draft as perfect as you can make it. When you have completed your final draft, you will need to proofread it. Proofreading involves looking very closely at all the details of your writing to make sure that there are no accidental or overlooked errors. Spelling and punctuation are some of the details to consider.

C. Sharing/Publishing

After evaluating the student essays for this chapter, your professor will remove names and make all of the papers available through closed reserve in the library (or another method). You should read all of your classmates' essays and vote for the one that you find provides the most effective evaluation. Your professor will count the votes and then provide copies of the two or three papers with the most votes to the director of the college's library. This student feedback will be helpful to the staff of the library in its efforts to meet standards and make improvements.

9.5 Extend

Additional Research—People are often content to hold onto misperceptions and mistakes, rather than do a little research to find out the facts. In the "Engage" section of this chapter, you explored the idea of a world language. What do you think are the five most commonly spoken languages in the world today, in order? What do you think are the five most commonly spoken native languages in the United States, in order? Write out your lists and then conduct research to find out the facts. How do your thoughts compare to the facts?

Thinking Skills—When we evaluate several items against the same standards with the goal of choosing the best one, we are making decisions. Like the evaluation process, the decision-making process follows certain steps:

The Decision Making Process—Step by Step

1. Carefully define the problem or situation that requires a decision.

2. Develop criteria (standards) for evaluating the alternatives (choices).

3. List the alternatives.

4. Check each alternative against the criteria.

5. Select the alternative that best meets the criteria.

Beyond the Classroom—Some organizations set standards and conduct evaluations to help people make better choices. The Association of College and Research Libraries (a part of the American Library Association) has established standards for college and university libraries. How do these standards compare to the standards you set in the "Explore" section of this chapter? Could you use the ACRL standards to help you make a more convincing evaluation?

Other organizations like the Consumers Union, which publishes *Consumer Reports*, or Web sites like CNET.com set benchmarks (another term for standards) and conduct evaluations of products to help consumers make better purchasing decisions. Still other organizations, magazines, Web sites, and retailers collect opinions of those who use a product or service and use those to provide ratings. (Keep in mind that these opinion-based evaluations do not usually establish standards and are based on softer, rather than firmer, evidence.)

Consult some of these rating sites to see what they would recommend to a college student interested in buying a laptop, to a professor looking for an LCD projector, or to a family looking for a family car.

Chapter 10—Problem and Solution

This chapter requires evaluation skills to identify problems and then puts creative problem-solving techniques to use in offering solutions in an essay form.

10.1 Engage—Improving Your College

In this activity, you will participate in identifying a problem on your campus and suggesting solutions.

In an effort to improve the programs, resources, and services it provides for its students, your college is setting up small focus groups to solicit input from students. You have been asked to participate on one of these groups. Your goal is to identify significant problems facing students and suggest possible solutions. Your views are especially important because they will provide an international student perspective.

Forming Groups: Divide the students into groups of three or four using a method that puts students together who have not already worked together.

1. In your groups, use brainstorming to come up with a list of problems you have noticed at your college. What are areas that should be improved? What is wrong with the college? Do not limit yourself. Consider all aspects of the programs, resources, and services. Consider academic issues, financial issues, and personal issues. Consider big-picture problems and small, day-to-day details. (Use 15 minutes.)

2. Now prioritize. Decide which five problems your group believes are the most significant. Rank them in order from the most significant to the fifth most significant. (Use 10 minutes.)

3. Together with your other group members, devise a solution for the problem you identified as the most significant. Decide what action your school should take to solve this problem. Be sure to explain exactly what needs to be done, who should do it, how it should be done. Address any of the other wh- questions that apply. You must include any cost associated with your solution, how this cost will be paid, and by whom. (Use 15 minutes.)

4. Choose someone from your group to mark off a portion of the blackboard (or whiteboard, or use a large piece of newsprint to hang on the wall) and write your list of the top five problems. Determine which two or three problems have been identified as the most significant for the whole class. Arrange to share this information with the appropriate college administrators. (Use 10 minutes.)

5. From all of the problems listed for the whole class, choose the one that you personally believe is the most important. Write two paragraphs; the first should explain the problem in detail and the second should explain your solution for the problem, including what, who, how, and any cost issues. (Use 15 minutes, or complete for homework.)

10.2 Explore—Creative Problem Solving

There are a number of mistakes that can be made in problem solving. Using the formal problem-solving process helps problem solvers to avoid making these mistakes. The problem-solving process includes the following steps:

1. Identify and clearly describe the problem. This includes answering the wh-questions related to the problem. It also includes establishing that there really is a problem and that it is worth solving.

2. Develop criteria for evaluating solutions. Just as with the evaluation process, it is important to set the standards that the best solution must meet before exploring solutions.

3. List possible solutions. An initial list can include numerous possibilities. It is important to avoid narrowing the possibilities too soon. It is also important to entertain creative, innovative solutions, to think outside the box.

4. Check each possible solution against the criteria. The criteria established in #2 above will help eliminate many of the possibilities and focus on the best. The criteria will also help avoid allowing biases to influence the choice of the best solution.

5. Select the solution that best meets the criteria.

Even problem solvers that use this process can miss some possible solutions because they find thinking in new and creative ways difficult. People often come up with the same old solutions because they are comfortable with the familiar. This approach limits the possible solutions and increases the potential for overlooking the best solution.

Search your library, a local bookstore, or the Internet for information on creative problem-solving techniques. These sources can show you ways to overcome thinking in the same old ways time after time. They usually provide examples of how techniques have been used to solve real-world problems. They also often use games and other activities to give readers practice in using the techniques.

Summarize one such problem-solving technique and/or activity and share it with your classmates. How does it fit with the process outlined above? How does it improve upon the process?

10.3 Explain—Problem-Solution Essay

As we saw in Chapter 9, people like to evaluate things. In the process of evaluating, both informally and formally, we often identify problems. In some cases, we have the power to solve these problems ourselves. In others, we have an opportunity to recommend solutions that can be carried out by others with the power to take action.

Identifying problems and recommending solutions happens informally all of the time. In our daily lives at home, at school, or at work, we are problem solvers. The problem-solving process and the problem-solution essay formalize this common practice to help make it more effective, both in identifying the best possible solution and in persuading others to take appropriate actions.

You learned about the formal problem-solving process in the previous section. In a problem-solution essay, you clearly describe in detail information from the key parts of that process.

Key Parts of the Problem-Solution Essay

A Clear Statement of the Problem—First, the writer must identify and describe the problem in enough detail to make clear to the readers the nature of the problem. The writer must also convince the readers that the problem is truly a problem and that it is possible and desirable to solve this problem.

A Summary of Possible Solutions—Second, the writer must demonstrate that he or she has explored a number of possible solutions to the problem (including, in some cases, not taking any action). When faced with problems, readers will naturally think of their own solutions. If the writer does not consider some of these possibilities, readers may be more likely to dismiss the best solution offered.

An Explanation of the Best Solution—Third, the writer needs to establish why this one solution is better than the others. As suggested in the "Engage" activity, the writer must take care to explain exactly what needs to be done, who should do it, and how it should be done. Also, he or she should include other information, especially any cost and who is responsible for paying the cost.

Related Structures

The Subjunctive

Some verbs and adjectives that express advice or requirements are followed by clauses with subjects whose verbs are in the simple form. This special use of the simple form of the verb is known as the **subjunctive**. The subjunctive form of a verb is required after certain expressions of advice. Examples of verbs in the subjunctive form are <u>underlined</u> below.

Verbs

advise—The students advise that the library <u>be</u> remodeled to include a cafe.
demand—The workers are demanding that their health insurance <u>be</u> extended.
insist—Professor Jones insists that his students <u>turn</u> their assignments in on time.

recommend—The committees recommend that the administration <u>provide</u> additional computer labs.

require—The college requires that each visitor <u>park</u> in a designated space.

suggest—I suggest that you <u>find</u> a more reliable source of information.

Adjectives

advisable—It is advisable that the college <u>make</u> these changes.

critical—It is critical that the government <u>take</u> action before it is too late.

crucial—It is crucial that the economy <u>show</u> signs of recovery soon.

essential—It is essential that students <u>have</u> the opportunity to use the latest technology.

imperative—It is imperative that you <u>improve</u> your grades.

mandatory—It is mandatory that no one <u>enter</u> the lab until the instructor is present.

necessary—It is necessary that the electricity <u>be</u> shut off during the renovation.

recommended—It is recommended that each student <u>back up</u> computer assignments.

suggested—It is suggested that this software <u>be used</u> because it is compatible with all platforms.

10.4 Exercise / Evaluate

Exercise 1: Warm-up Writing

In many of the world's cities, traffic has become a terrible problem, creating what is called gridlock (cars cannot move). In a paragraph (10-12 sentences), first describe a bad traffic problem from your experience, and then offer a solution. Recommend a solution that is feasible and affordable.

Exercise 2: Related Structure

For each of the problems given below, recommend a solution in a complete sentence using the word in parentheses.

For example: economic aid (require)—The World Bank requires that economic aid be tied to balanced budgets.

1. endangered species (advise)

2. homelessness (recommend)

3. hunger (suggest)

4. illegal immigration (advisable)

5. illiteracy (critical)

6. malaria (crucial)

7. nuclear and chemical weapons (essential)

8. oil spills (imperative)

9. overpopulation (necessary)

10. pollution (recommended)

11. poor water quality (suggested)

12. rain forest destruction (advise)

13. refugees (critical)

14. slavery (crucial)

15. technology gap between rich and poor countries (essential)

16. terrorism (imperative)

17. third world debt (mandatory)

18. war (necessary)

Exercise 3: Focused Writing

Choose three of the problems from the Exercise 2 above and for each write a four-sentence mini-paragraph. The first two sentences should identify and explain the problem in as much detail as possible. The last two sentences should give your solution, including who should carry out the solution and how.

Exercise 4: Problem-Solution Essay Assignment

In this assignment, you will practice what you have learned about the problem-solving process and the problem-solution essay. You will use this type of writing to share your good ideas for improvement and to influence action. For this reason, problem-solution writing can be a useful and powerful tool.

Keep in mind that the body of this essay has three main parts—a clear statement of the problem, a summary of possible solutions, and an explanation of the best or recommended solution. For the most part, you will be describing an existing problem, so you will use verbs in the present tense. However, remember that after certain verbs and adjectives like those listed above in the "Related Structures" section, you will have to use the subjunctive form of the verb, a special use of the simple form. Informal recommendations often use the second-person pronoun (you), but in this more formal writing, it would be more appropriate to use third-person pronouns (he, she, it, they) as your subjects.

Improving Your College. Choose one of the problems that you and your classmates identified in the "Engage" activity above. Write one sentence in which you identify the problem and state the solution that you will recommend. This will serve as your working thesis statement. (With your professor's approval, you may want to choose an alternative as the focus of your essay, one of the world problems you explored in Exercise 2 above.)

Use your working thesis statement to guide your gathering and organization of evidence. Use this information to write a five-to-seven paragraph problem-solution essay. Your audience is everyone at your school, but especially those with the power to take the action necessary to solve the problem. Your purpose is to influence action to improve your college.

Using the Writing Process

Follow the steps of the writing process spelled out below to help complete your essay.

I. Before Writing

A. Getting Ideas—SWOT Analysis (Strengths, Weaknesses, Opportunities, Threats)

In order to make a convincing case that your recommendation is the best solution for the identified problem, you will need to establish the good qualities and address the bad qualities of your recommendation. One way of gathering and organizing information, both good and bad, about your solution is to use SWOT analysis. Business and educational organizations often use this tool in evaluating their programs, resources, and services and making improvements.

Strengths—What are the strengths, or advantages, of your solution?

Weaknesses—What are the weaknesses, or disadvantages, of your solution?

Opportunities—What support is available for your solution from others?

Threats—What obstacles or opposition will your solution face?

_____

II. During Writing

A. Planning

Use the following essay template to help plan your writing.

Essay Template

Your name: _____   Audience: _____

Professor's name: _____   Purpose: _____

Course name: _____   Essay type: <u>Problem-Solution</u>

Date: _____   Source: _____

Title: _____

Introduction

Invitation (complete sentence):

Orientation (notes; include information about why the intended audience would be interested in this general topic):

Thesis statement (complete sentence; include a clear indication that the essay is a problem-solution essay):

Body

Clear Statement of the Problem—Topic sentence (complete sentence):

<u>Firm evidence (notes)</u>   <u>Soft evidence (notes)</u>

Summary of Possible Solutions—Topic sentence (complete sentence):

<u>Firm evidence (notes)</u>   <u>Soft evidence (notes)</u>

Explanation of the Best Solution—Topic sentence (complete sentence):

Firm evidence (notes)   Soft evidence (notes)

Conclusion

Transition (word, phrase, or none):

Restatement of thesis statement (complete sentence):

Summary of main points (notes):

Final thought (complete sentence):

Initial Impression

Strengths of the essay:

Weaknesses of the essay:

Actions needed to address weaknesses:

II. During Writing (continued)

B. Writing

Use the writing strategy that you believe will work best for this essay. You can use One Step after Another, Body First, Outside In, Microcosm, Whatever Works, or another strategy of your own or someone else's design.

III. After Writing

A. Reviewing

1. Self-Review. Your mentor will be reviewing and evaluating your writing with the questions from the "Review/Evaluation Guide" in mind. You should ask the same questions of yourself so that you can make the changes necessary before giving your writing to your mentor for review.

Review/Evaluation Guide

I—Ideas and Information

1. Is the main idea of the writing clear (topic and focus)?
2. Does the evidence provided relate to the thesis of the essay and/or the topic of the paragraph (unity)?
3. Is the objective evidence adequate to meet the requirements of the writing context?
4. If used, is the subjective evidence appropriate to the writing context?
5. Are the ideas and information presented accurate and reliable? and correctly attributed?

O—Organization

1. Does the organization of the writing follow the guidelines for an essay or other type of writing?
2. Is the organization appropriate to the rhetorical form(s) used?
3. Are paragraphs organized according to appropriate guidelines?
4. Does the organization (both essay and paragraph) support the logical development of the thesis?
5. Are transitions and repetition used effectively to link the elements of the writing (coherence)?

S—Sentence Structure

1. Are all of the sentences complete? Are simple, compound, and complex sentences correctly structured?
2. Are the verb tenses appropriate?

3. Do all subjects and verbs agree in number? Do all nouns and pronouns agree in number and gender?
4. Are modifiers appropriately linked to the words they modify?
5. Do words, phrases, and clauses follow the guidelines for sentence order and parallelism?

W—Word Use

1. Are the correct content words used?
2. Are the correct word forms used?
3. Are the words used appropriate to the writing context in terms of register, formality, and level of specificity?
4. Are the correct function words used?
5. Are all words spelled correctly?

P—Punctuation Plus

1. Is the manuscript format appropriate to the writing context?
2. Does the paper meet any required style guidelines?
3. Are sections (if used) and paragraphs set off appropriately (indenting and spacing)?
4. Is sentence punctuation correct? Are full stops (. ? !), dividers (, ; : — ( )), and others (" " ...) used correctly?
5. Is word punctuation correct? Are apostrophes, hyphens, capital letters, italics, abbreviations, and numbers used correctly?

III. After Writing (continued)

B. Finishing

Rewrite as needed, using feedback from the review. Pay special attention to the use of modals of advice and expressions requiring the subjunctive mood.

Proofread with an eye on sentence and word punctuation. You may want to consult a writer's handbook for detailed explanation of both types of punctuation.

C. Sharing/Publishing

After you have finished your problem-solution essay, you should share it with the intended audience, those with the power to put your solution into practice.

10.5 Extend

Thinking Skills—In the "Explore" section, you learned five steps in the problem-solving process. These steps are only one of many ways of looking at problem solving, creative thinking, and the related idea of intelligence. In your library, local bookstores, and on the Internet, you can find many sources on these topics. Some authors whose writing you might find of interest include:

James L. Adams—Among other topics, Adams explores how people's perceptions, culture, environment, emotions, intellect, and communication skills can create barriers to problem solving.

Edward de Bono—De Bono has done a great deal of work in the area of creative thinking strategies and how to teach these strategies so that people can improve their problem solving.

Howard Gardner—Based on his research into human intelligence, Gardner has developed the idea of multiple intelligences. This human attribute has more than one dimension, Gardner believes, and by exploring the seven or eight facets of intelligence, people can exploit their strengths and overcome their weaknesses.

If you wish to move beyond the overview of thinking skills presented in this book, you may want to look into the work of these or other experts in the fields of problem solving, creative thinking, and intelligence.

Beyond the Classroom—Everywhere scientists, policy makers, activists, governments, and organizations are involved in identifying the world's problems and taking action to solve these problems. You can see what the United Nations is doing to address world issues at its Web site <www.un.org>.

World problems do attract a lot of attention. However, because trying to grasp these big-picture problems can be overwhelming for one person or small groups, many activists have suggested that individuals should "think globally, but act locally."

Conduct some research on the community near your college. Determine which local problems are the most serious. Find out who is working to solve these problems and what they have done. What would you recommend should be done to solve these local problems? How can you help to bring about these solutions?

Many colleges and universities now include service-learning programs that encourage students to combine their academic interests with community service. Does your school have such a program and does it help students act locally to solve problems?

Using Technology—Software developers interested in improving problem solving and creative thinking have created products for computers that help users progress step-by-step from problem through solution. Do some research to find one of these products. Who is the audience for this software? What is its purpose? How does it work? Would it be useful to you? Share your findings with your classmates.

Chapter 11—Cause and Effect

This chapter introduces causal relationships and provides practice in writing essays that describe these relationships.

11.1 Engage—Foreign Study

This activity gives you an opportunity to draw on your experience to identify both positive and negative effects.

World events regularly cause the United States government and American universities to take a new look at the idea of foreign study. The debate about foreign study has also been an issue in many other countries besides the United States. There are and always have been advantages and disadvantages to going abroad to study. What are the advantages and disadvantages of foreign study?

Forming Groups: Divide the students into groups of three or four. Assign half of the groups the student's perspective. Assign the other half the countries' perspective.

1. For those with student's perspective, address the question: What are the advantages and disadvantages to foreign study for the students? For those with the countries' perspective, address the question: What are the advantages and disadvantages to foreign study for the homeland that the students are leaving? What are the advantages and disadvantages for the countries where these students go to study? (Use 20 minutes.)

2. In your groups, rank the advantages from most important to the least important. Also rank the disadvantages from most important to least important. (Use 10 minutes.)

3. Bring your group together with a group that explored the other perspective (student perspective with country perspective). Share your ideas. Add these new ideas to your list. Together, both groups should choose the four most important advantages and four most important disadvantages to foreign study. (Use 20 minutes.)

4. Choose the statement that you agree with: Foreign study is a good idea for several reasons. OR Foreign study is not a good idea for several reasons. Start with the statement you chose and write two or three good paragraphs to explain why you agree with the statement you chose. (Use 45 minutes in class or for homework.)

11.2 Explore—Cause, Correlation, and Coincidence

Events that occur in a sequence (one after another) can have a number of different relationships. In your discussion of the advantages and disadvantages of study in a foreign country, you were looking at effects—the effects (both positive and negative) of studying in a foreign country. When you analyze two (or more) events that occur in a sequence, the strongest relationship between those two events is a **cause-and-effect** relationship. If one event leads directly to another event, we have a cause-and-effect relationship. Mary throws her banana peel on the ground instead of in the garbage can. Bob slips on the banana peel. He falls. He lands on his hand. He breaks his finger. He experiences a lot of pain. In this case, Mary's littering leads directly to Bob's accident, which leads through other events in a cause-and-effect chain to a trip to the doctor.

Another type of relationship between two events that occur in a sequence is **correlation**. There is a correlation between two events when they always or often happen together, but there is no clear cause-and-effect relationship between them. There may be a cause-and-effect relationship that we do not have enough evidence to prove; or, the two events may share the same cause. For example, people in the United States who buy more heavy coats also use more heating oil. The coats do not cause the heating oil use and the heating oil use does not cause the purchase of more heavy coats. Actually, the cold weather causes both, and these things are related because they have the same cause.

A third type of relationship between two events that occur in a sequence is **coincidence**. A coincidence occurs when two events have no clear relationship. There is no correlation and there is no cause-and-effect. For example, the doorbell rings and your friend sneezes. The doorbell did not cause the sneeze. If you rang the doorbell 50 times, your friend would not sneeze 50 times or even 20 times.

Practice. Decide whether each of the following pairs represents a Cause-Effect, Correlation, or Coincidence relationship.

Lightning—>friends arrive
Lightning—>lights go off
Lightning—>phone rings
Lightning—>rain
Lightning—>thunder

Smoking—>ambulance passing
Smoking—>children of smokers smoke
Smoking—>increase in coffee drinking
Smoking—>increase in heart rate
Smoking—>watering eyes

Activity. Read the following events and decide if they are Cause-Effect, Correlation, or Coincidence. Write the appropriate relationship next to the events.

full moon and increased crime

smoking and drug use

drug use and crime

full moon and high tide

rock-and-roll and drug use

full moon and bright night

gender and career

television and violence

growth in Internet and growth in the economy

astrological sign and personality

birth order and personality

academic major and lifespan

gender and lifespan

academic major and wealth

country of origin and native language

cars and air pollution

cars and teenage pregnancy

smoking and lung cancer

smoking and interest in soccer

age and maternity

age and health problems

growth in Internet and fall of the Berlin Wall

gender and hair color

growth in Internet and phone line traffic

country of origin and left-handedness

11.3 Explain—Cause-Effect Essay

Humans like to know why things happen. They like to know the results of actions. They are interested in causes and effects. They cannot do anything about actions that are coincidental, but there is a feeling that establishing a cause-effect relationship gives a person power to change actions and outcomes. The cause-effect essay provides a way for a writer to explore causes and effects, to share the power to change outcomes with others.

Cause-effect relationships can often be quite complicated. Some things happen for many reasons. Actions have many results. Some actions lead to other actions, which lead to other actions, which lead to other actions, and so on. To avoid becoming too complicated, cause and effect essays must stay focused. In addition to other focusing tools, cause-effect essays usually include one of the following:

Focus on causes—Essays with this focus choose a single happening and explore the several reasons why it happened. They explore the causes of an event.
Focus on effects—Essays with this focus choose a single action and explore the several results of this action. They focus on the effects of the action.
Cause and effect chain—Essays with this focus follow a single thread of actions. Each action is the result of the action that came before it and the reason for the action that follows it.

Focus on Causes

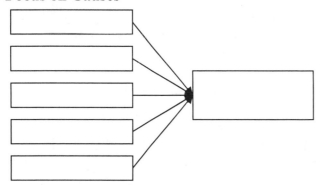

Focus on Effects

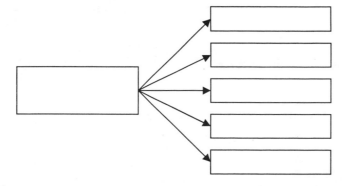

Cause and Effect Chain

Related Structures

Cause and Effect Expressions

There are a number of phrase markers, clause markers, and transition words that can be used to express cause-effect relationships. For the most part, these expressions mean <u>because</u> or <u>therefore</u>.

Used in <u>cause</u> phrases—because of. Other expressions that are synonyms for *because of*—as a result of, by virtue of, due to, on account of.

Used in <u>cause</u> clauses—because. Other expressions that are synonyms for *because*—as, due to the fact that, inasmuch as, in that, now that (= because now), since. The word *for* (meaning because) can also be used in compound sentences. Keep in mind that *for* has other functions; it usually is a preposition.

Used in <u>effect</u> clauses—therefore. Other expressions that are synonyms for *therefore*—as a result, consequently, for this reason, hence, thus. The word *so* can also be used in compound sentences.

Examples:

<u>Because of</u> the richness of their native cultures and their different experiences, international students improve the academic and social life of the colleges they attend.
OR
International students improve the academic and social life of the colleges they attend <u>because of</u> the richness of their native cultures and their different experiences.

(Other expressions—as a result of, by virtue of, due to, on account of—could be substituted for *<u>because of</u>*.)

<u>Because</u> international students bring the richness of their native cultures and their different experiences, they improve the academic and social life of the colleges they attend.
OR
International students improve the academic and social life of the colleges they attend <u>because</u> they bring the richness of their native cultures and their different experiences.

(Other expressions—as, due to the fact that, inasmuch as, in that, since—could be substituted for because.)

International students improve the academic and social life of the colleges they attend, <u>for</u> they bring their native cultures and their different experiences. (The word <u>for</u> is a coordinating conjunction and must come between two independent clauses; it cannot appear at the beginning of a sentence.)

International students bring the richness of their native cultures and their different experiences. <u>Therefore</u>, they improve the academic and social life of the colleges they attend.
OR
International students bring the richness of their native cultures and their different experiences; <u>therefore</u>, they improve the academic and social life of the colleges they attend.

(Other expressions—as a result, consequently, for this reason, hence, thus—could be substituted for <u>therefore</u>. Therefore and its synonyms are transition words and must be used between two complete sentences, either after a period or semicolon. A comma must follow the transition words.)

International students bring the richness of their native cultures and their different experiences, <u>so</u> they enrich the academic and social life of the colleges they attend. (The word <u>so</u> is a coordinating conjunction and must come between two independent clauses; it cannot appear at the beginning of a sentence.)

Verbs that Express Correlation and Cause-Effect

Some verbs are especially useful when establishing correlation or cause-effect relationships.

Correlation—tend to + verb; correlates with + noun or gerund
Cause-effect—cause + noun or gerund; lead to + noun or gerund

Examples:

Men <u>tend to</u> die younger than women.
Studies show that the choice of a career in the arts <u>correlates with</u> a shorter lifespan.

The nicotine in cigarette smoke <u>causes</u> an immediate increase in the heart rate and blood pressure of the smoker.
A gene inherited from their mothers <u>leads to</u> baldness in men.

Causative Verbs

There are a few verbs that when used in a special way with other verbs express a cause-effect relationship. These verbs are called **causative verbs**. They are synonyms for "cause someone/something to do something" (cause + object + to + verb). They are also synonyms for "force someone/something to do something" or "require someone/something to do something" (force + object + to + verb or require + object + to + verb).

The structure used with causative verbs is: causative + object + verb (in simple form). The verbs make and have can be used as causatives.

For example:

Regular verbs

The airline caused the student to check his large backpack.
The airline forced the student to check his large backpack.
The airline required the student to check his large backpack.

Causative verbs

The airline made the student check his large backpack. (Note, to should not be included.)
The airline had the student check his large backpack. (Note, to should not be included.)

11.4 Exercise / Evaluation

Exercise 1: Warm-up Writing

In many countries and cultures, including American culture, it is common for young people to leave their hometown and move to a large city. Explain the main reasons (causes) why this is true in your country, or why it is not true in your country. Choose the three or four main reasons and write a paragraph of 10-12 sentences.

Exercise 2: Related Structures

Drawing on what you learned in the "Explore" and "Related Structures" sections above, choose the best expression from the following choices to complete these sentences.

A. Choose the appropriate word—either because or so (use a comma before so).

Example: Jack forgot his keys, so he was unable to get into his house.

1. The Holman Manor lost part of its roof in the thunderstorm _____ much of its beautiful antique furniture was damaged by water.

2. Much of its beautiful antique furniture was damaged by water _____ the Holman Manor lost part of its roof in the thunderstorm.

3. His children had an increased risk of health problems _____ the man smoked several packs of cigarettes a day.

4. The man smoked several packs of cigarettes a day _____ his children had an increased risk of health problems.

5. _____ cable television offers hundreds of channels, fewer people watch the three original television networks.

6. Fewer people watch the three original television networks _____ cable television offers hundreds of channels.

7. More couples are divorced than fifty years ago _____ more children grow up with only one parent.

8. Many international students adjust to and feel quite comfortable with their new surroundings _____ they experience anxiety when they have to return to their homeland.

9. A number of scientists are convinced that world temperatures are rising _____ the gases created by modern industry have created a greenhouse effect.

10. _____ modern Americans have readily available transportation and sedentary jobs, they burn far fewer calories than their grandparents.

B. Choose the appropriate verb—either <u>correlates with</u> (correlation) or <u>leads to</u> (cause-effect).

Example: Police records fail to support the idea that an increase in crime <u>correlates with</u> a full moon.

1. Studies show that smoking _____ an increased likelihood of hard drug use.

2. Drug addiction _____ other criminal activities.

3. The passing of the moon overhead _____ a rise in the ocean tides.

4. The increase in the use of cars and truck has _____ an increase in pollution.

5. The growth in the use of the Internet has _____ growth in the traffic on phone lines and cables.

6. Gender _____ lifespan.

7. Exposure to high levels of radiation _____ problems in internal organ functioning.

8. Psychologists maintain that personality type _____ birth order.

9. Astrologers claim that the position of the sun, moon, and stars at people's times of birth _____ the events of their lives, but scientists have not proven this.

10. Left-handedness does not _____ an increased probability that a person will have a leadership role.

Exercise 3: Focused Writing Practice

For each of the topics listed below, try to list five of the most important causes and five of the most important effects. Then, choose two of the topics and write a paragraph for each. Your paragraph may focus on causes OR on effects.

Causes	Topic	Effects
1.	immigration	1.
2.		2.
3.		3.
4.		4.
5.		5.

Causes	Topic	Effects
1.	divorce	1.
2.		2.
3.		3.
4.		4.
5.		5.

Causes	Topic	Effects
1.	obesity	1.
2.		2.
3.		3.
4.		4.
5.		5.

Causes	Topic	Effects
1.	pollution	1.
2.		2.
3.		3.
4.		4.
5.		5.

Causes	Topic	Effects
1.	success	1.
2.		2.
3.		3.
4.		4.
5.		5.

Exercise 4: Cause-Effect Essay Assignment

In this assignment, you will have the opportunity to use the ideas you have already developed to write a cause-effect essay. Remember, cause-effect essays allow you to explore two (or more) events that occur in a sequence and establish a causal relationship between them. Establishing a positive cause-effect relationship can give readers an idea of how to pursue a beneficial outcome. For example, if using certain mnemonic devices improves grades on vocabulary tests, students should employ them in their studies. Establishing a negative cause-effect relationship can allow readers to find ways to avoid negative consequences. For example, if eating certain types of fish increases the incidence of mercury poisoning, people can choose other fish.

Typically, cause-effect essays use third-person subjects. They use present tense to establish general cause-effect relationships, past tense to explain cause-effect relationships that have occurred in history, and future tense to explore effects that can be anticipated from current events.

Establishing a Cause or Effect Relationship

Choose the topic from the "Engage" activity or one of the topics from Exercise 3 (or another topic acceptable to your professor) and develop it into a cause-effect essay. Using the thesis statement that you have developed, the information you gathered above, and other evidence you can gather, write a five-to-seven-paragraph essay. The purpose for your writing is to provide information that can be useful to those people you have identified as your audience.

Using the Writing Process

Follow the steps of the writing process spelled out below to help complete your essay.

I. Before Writing

A. Getting Ideas—Secondary Research

In your library, at a bookstore, or on the Internet, you should be able to find information to supplement the ideas that you have gathered for your cause-effect essay. Because this information is based on the observations, experiments, interviews, and efforts of other people (not your own direct efforts), this information is secondary research. Secondary research allows a writer to provide evidence beyond his or her own experience. Even so, keep in mind that secondary research is a supplement to your own work, not a substitute for it.

B. Grouping Ideas

Use one of the diagrams from the "Explain" section above to group your ideas. In each box, include details under each cause (or effect)—facts and statistics, observations, records, expert testimony, and other evidence—that proves the relationship.

II. During Writing

A. Planning—Use the sentence outline sheet below to plan and outline your essay.

_____

Sentence Outline

Your name: _____   Audience: _____

Professor's name: _____   Purpose: _____

Course name: _____   Essay type: _____

Date: _____   Source: _____

Title: _____

I. Introduction

A. Write your invitation here. Write a complete sentence.

What type of invitation did you choose? A quotation, a question, a surprising comment, a brief definition, a general statement of fact, an explanation of the topic's importance, an explanation of the topic's timeliness, an appeal to common experience, an anecdote—a brief story related to the topic.

B. What background information (history, news story, interesting fact, statistics, other), if any, should your reader have as orientation to the topic? Describe that information here in one sentence.

C. What is your thesis? Write a complete sentence here. Remember: (1) use focusing tools to clarify the topic of the essay; (2) make the topic of your essay the subject of your sentence; (3) be specific but not too specific; (4) include a preview of your subtopics in the order that you will develop them. Your thesis should clearly state if your evaluation is positive or negative.

II. Body

A. Do you need to include an extended background section here? What information will this section contain? Summarize your ideas in one sentence.

B. Write the topic sentence for your 1st cause (or effect) subtopic here. Write a complete sentence. Use coherence techniques to link this subtopic to your thesis.

1. What objective evidence will you use to develop this subtopic? Summarize in one complete sentence the facts, statistics, expert testimony, observations, and/or records that you will use.

2. What subjective evidence will you use to develop this subtopic? Summarize in one complete sentence the analogies, precedents, opinions, and/or experience that you will use.

C. Write the topic sentence for your 2nd cause (or effect) subtopic here. Write a complete sentence. Use coherence techniques to link this subtopic to your thesis.

1. What objective evidence will you use to develop this subtopic? Summarize in one complete sentence the facts, statistics, expert testimony, observations, and/or records that you will use.

2. What subjective evidence will you use to develop this subtopic? Summarize in one complete sentence the analogies, precedents, opinions, and/or experience that you will use.

3. Repeat 1 and 2 for additional cause (or effect) subtopics, if needed.

III. Conclusion

A. What kind of transition will you use to help the reader go from the body to the conclusion?

B. What has the reader learned about your topic? Restate your thesis in new words. Write one complete sentence here.

C. Write a summary of your subtopics in one complete sentence here.

D. Give your reader something to think about as s/he leaves your paper. Write a resolution or final thought here. Make it a complete sentence. What type of resolution will you use? (What type of resolution did you choose? A quotation, a question, a surprising comment, a brief definition, a general statement of fact, an explanation of the topic's importance, an explanation of the topic's timeliness, an appeal to common experience, an anecdote—a brief story related to the topic)

II. *During Writing* (continued)

B. Writing

Use the writing strategy that you believe will work best for this essay. You can use One Step after Another, Body First, Outside In, Microcosm, Whatever Works, or another strategy of your own or someone else's design.

III. *After Writing*

A. Reviewing

1. <u>Self-Review.</u> Use the Review/Evaluation Guide in the "Extra" section to guide your review.

2. <u>Peer Review.</u> Exchange your cause-effect essay with a classmate. Each of you will read the other's essay and then complete the "Responding to a First Draft" for that paper. Try to be as detailed as possible in answering the questions. Your feedback will help your classmate make improvements to her/his first draft.

Responding to a First Draft

Answer the following questions with as much detail as you can. Answering these questions will require you to show that you understand what is being done in the paper.

General

1. What is the title? It should give an idea of the main idea of the paper.

2. Who is the main intended audience? Who should read this essay? Check one.
_____General readers   _____Specific groups   _____Experts
_____The writer's peers   _____One specific person   _____The writer her/himself

3. What is the main purpose? (check one)
_____Share or Express   _____Inform or Explain   _____Prove or Persuade

4. What form is used primarily? (check one)
___Narrative   ___Process   ___Classification and Division
___Description   ___Comparison and Contrast   ___Evaluation
___Cause and Effect   ___Problem and Solution

Introduction

5. Does the paper have an introductory paragraph? If not, how is the reader oriented to the information presented?

6. The Invitiation. How is the reader's interest in this paper attracted? (check one)
___a funny story   ___a difficult question   ___a famous quotation
___a challenge   ___a similar or different experience ___something new
___something old in a new light   ___a statement of general interest

7. What is the thesis statement? (main idea sentence)

8. How was the general topic focused? (Check all that apply.)
___time   ___place   ___number or sequence   ___category or characteristic
___similarity/difference   ___quality   ___cause/effect   ___problem/solution

Body

9. What are the three to five main points developed in the body of the paper?

10. Do they support the thesis statement? How?

11. Are there points that could be added or removed? What are they?

12. What forms of evidence have been used? (Check all that apply.)
___facts and statistics   ___observations   ___records   ___expert testimony
___precedents   ___analogies   ___experience   ___opinions

13. Is the evidence adequate to convince the readers? If not, what should be done?

Conclusion

14. Is there a concluding paragraph? If not, how is the reader reminded of the key points?

15. Which of the following is included in the conclusion? (Check all that apply.)
_____a restatement of thesis   _____a summary of main points
_____a famous quotation related to thesis   _____a call to action

16. Does the paper give a feeling of completeness? If not, what is missing, and what should be done?

Sentence Structure, Word Use, and Punctuation

17. Carefully check each of the following items to assure that as many mistakes as possible have been corrected.

___complete sentences   ___appropriate verb tenses   ___uses transitions
___subject/verb agreement   ___correct word forms   ___spelling
___correct word order   ___capitals and full stops   ___format
___modifiers correctly located

Plan for Second Draft

18. What questions need to be answered before the next draft? What changes need to be made?

_____

III. After Writing (continued)

B. Finishing

Rewrite as needed, using feedback from the review. Carefully examine the relationships that you discuss in the essay to assure that you have established a cause-effect connection and not merely highlighted a coincidence. Review your use of cause-effect expressions for correct meaning and grammar.

Proofread to be sure that manuscript format, style, paragraphing, and punctuation are all correct.

C. Sharing/Publishing

After you have finished your cause-effect essay, you should share it with the intended audience. If you wrote about the advantages to having international students at your college or university (positive effects), you should share your essay with the student newspaper or with college administrators.

11.5 Extend

Thinking Skills—In the "Explore" section of this chapter, you learned about three relationships between events that occur in a sequence: cause-and-effect, correlation, and coincidence. People often make mistakes in their judgment about which relationship applies to a specific set of events. When these mistakes are in informal, unimportant situations, they generally do not cause any harm. However, when people use mistaken causal relationships to influence the opinions or actions of others, they create problems. In extreme cases, these problems include unfairly playing with people's emotions and fears as well as wasting their time and money. Mistaken causal relationships or false causes take a few common forms:

Coincidence is presented as cause—Two events that occur in a sequence often have no relationship but chance. For example, the doorbell rings and your friend sneezes. If you then tell your brother not to ring the doorbell because you don't want your friend to sneeze, your use of a mistaken causal relationship does little harm. If a superstitious athlete decides that she must wear a certain pair of socks in the Olympics because she was wearing those socks when she broke the world record, she is using a mistaken causal relationship, but her incorrect judgment will probably cause no harm. However, in some cases—when a gambler bets heavily on tails in the toss of a coin because the previous twenty tosses came up heads; when a police investigation focuses prematurely on one suspect who happened to be in the area at the time of the crime; when an ancient culture sacrifices a virgin to assure a productive harvest—money, time, even lives can be lost.

Correlation is presented as cause—Two events in a sequence have a correlation when their occurrence together is greater than the statistical expectation for chance. The more this occurrence exceeds chance, the greater the correlation. However, the fact that events are correlated does not mean they have a cause-and-effect relationship. There may not be enough information to establish confidently a cause-and-effect relationship. The situation may be too complex to clearly link the two events in any definitive way. The two events may share a common cause, close or distant.

Effect is presented as cause—Two events may have a cause-and-effect relationship, but if they occur extremely close in sequence or it is not clear when one occurs with respect to the other, the effect may be mistaken for the cause. For example, we know that a fired rifle causes the hole in the target even if we see the hole before we hear evidence that the gun was fired. But, it is not immediately clear if participation in violent sports causes violent social behavior or if a predisposition to violent social behavior leads to participation in violent sports.

These mistaken causal relationships are just one set of logical fallacies. **Logical fallacies** are types of faulty reasoning. When they are used to prove a point, promote a policy, or persuade someone to take action, these fallacies provide a shaky foundation for the argument, a foundation that will eventually collapse and undermine the purpose of the writing. Unfortunately, faulty reasoning can work as long as people lack adequate knowledge of the issues, they are easily fooled, or they are ignorant. Search your library, local bookstore, or the Internet for information about logical fallacies and logical fallacies in the media.

Chapter 12—The Research Paper

This chapter provides practice writing a document based primarily on sources of information outside the writer, especially sources available in the college library.

12.1 Engage—Plagiarism

This activity is designed to help you find out more about a serious problem related to writing research papers—plagiarism.

Plagiarism is a complicated issue that poses problems for students and scholars already familiar with the standards of research writing in the United States. It is especially challenging for students new to the United States to understand and avoid this problem.

Part 1

Forming Groups: Divide Students into four research groups. Each group should receive one set of questions below to research.

Unlike most of the other "Engage" activities, you will complete Part 1 of this activity outside of class using the Internet. Conduct an online search to find information that answers the following questions. You need only answer the set of questions assigned to your group. The <u>underlined</u> words may be helpful as search terms.

Group 1—What is <u>plagiarism</u>? What are the different levels or <u>types of plagiarism</u>?

Group 2—How can students appropriately conduct <u>scholarly research</u>? What techniques should be used to <u>avoid plagiarism</u>? What is meant by <u>attributing sources</u>?

Group 3—What are some examples of <u>plagiarism in the news</u>? According to these recent news stories, <u>who has committed plagiarism</u>?

Group 4—<u>Technology and plagiarism</u>: How is technology being used to make it easier to commit plagiarism and to make it easier to catch plagiarists? What are <u>essay mills</u> or <u>research paper mills</u>? What <u>plagiarism software</u> is available?

Part 2

In class, students should be regrouped into collaboration groups of four or more with at least one representative from each of the four research groups.

After completing the research outside of class, you will share you findings with your classmates. The representatives of Group 1 should share first, Group 2 second, and so on. You will want to take notes on what you learn. You will need them for Part 3.

Part 3—Write one paragraph summarizing everything you learned about plagiarism.

12.2 Explore—Library Research

Libraries provide their patrons with many different types of information from a variety of sources. Understanding the nature of these sources, their intended use, as well as their strengths and weaknesses is important for writers. Nowadays, libraries offer access to both print and electronic sources. Below are some commonly used sources.

A. Print Sources
   1. General Reference Sources
      a. Encyclopedias
      b. Almanacs
      c. Atlases
      d. Statistical abstracts

   2. Books

   3. Periodicals
      a. Academic and scholarly journals
      b. Popular magazines
      c. Newspapers

   4. Other Texts—booklets, pamphlets, reports, circulars

   5. Graphics—maps, charts, tables, posters

B. Electronic Sources
   1. Audio-Visual Sources
      a. Analog
      b. Digital

   2. Electronic Databases
      a. CD-ROM and other on-site media
      b. Off-site databases accessible through the Internet

   3. Worldwide Web

Activity

This activity provides you practice finding research sources in the library and collecting the information you need to attribute and document your sources. You will need to spend at least an hour in the library.

For each type of source listed, find information about the topic assigned to you by your instructor. (Possible topics include divorce, homelessness, hunger, immigration, obesity, overpopulation, pollution, technology, and others such as those listed in Chapter 10.) Collect the details required about each source you find.

Research Source Guide

Topic: _____

A. Print Sources
    1. General Reference Sources
        a. Encyclopedia title: _____

            Year published (copyright): _____

            Article (or entry) title from the encyclopedia: _____

            Page numbers of the article: _____

        b. Almanac title: _____

            Year published (copyright): _____

            Edition number (if available): _____

            City of publication: _____

            Publishing company: _____

            Page numbers of the information: _____

    2. Book
        Author or editor: Last name—_____

                          First name—_____

                          Middle initial (if available)—_____

        Title: _____

        Year published (copyright): _____

        Edition number (if available): _____

City of publication: _____

Publishing company: _____

Page numbers of the information: _____

3. Periodical

Author of article (if available): Last name—_____

First name—_____

Middle initial (if available)—_____

Article title: _____

Periodical title: _____

Volume and number (scholarly journal): Vol.—_____; no.—_____

Date of publication (popular magazine or newspaper): _____

Page numbers of article: _____

B. Electronic Sources

2. Electronic Database

a or b. CD-ROM or Off-site database available through the Internet

Author of article (if available): Last name—_____

First name—_____

Middle initial (if available)—_____

Article title: _____

Periodical title: _____

Volume and number (scholarly journal): Vol.—_____; no.—_____

Date of publication (popular magazine or newspaper): _____

Page numbers of article: _____

Title of the database: _____

Publisher of the database: _____

Date of the database: _____

Internet address (if accessed through the Internet): _____

3. Worldwide Web

Author of Web page or Web article (if available):

Last name—_____

First name—_____

Middle initial (if available)—_____

Web page or Web article title: _____

Web site title: _____

Company or organization providing Web site (if available): _____

Date of last Web page/site update: _____

Date of your visit: _____

Internet address: _____

12.3. Explain—The Research Paper

Essays allow writers to explore their own knowledge and experience, and to share them with readers. For the most part, the main source for the information presented is the writer her- or himself. In some cases, the essay writer may need to fill gaps in personal knowledge or experience by consulting other people or other sources of information. However, the foundation for the essay and the majority of the information it expresses is the writer.

Research papers allow writers to explore topics about which they have little knowledge and with which they have little experience. So, the research paper writer must gather information from other sources. Either the writer must conduct primary research—surveys, interviews, discussions, experiments, or other research activities—to find out the unknown information, or the writer must consult others who have conducted such research (secondary research). These others may be individual experts, groups, corporations, or governments. They may share the information through conversations or personal correspondence, but most often they share the information through documents published in periodicals, books, online sites, or other written sources.

In using information from other sources, a writer faces a number of challenges.

Evaluation of sources—In gathering information for a research paper, a writer must assess certain characteristics of the sources to determine how appropriate and valuable they are. Sources are **trustworthy** if they have information provided by people qualified in the field using accepted methods of research. Sources are **reliable** if their information has also been found correct by other sources. Sources are **timely** if they have been created at a time recent enough so that the information has not changed. Sources are **deep** if the information they provide is sufficiently detailed and seriously treated.

Evaluation of evidence—Review Chapter 4 for an explanation of evaluating evidence.

Adaptation of information—The goal of a research paper is not simply to reproduce one source created by an expert in the field, nor is it to cut blocks of research from other sources and connect them together into a collection of expert views. The research paper writer must begin with a thesis, find information to support that thesis, and adapt that information into a document that has support, unity, and coherence. Adapting this information may involve quoting certain passages, paraphrasing others, and summarizing still others. (See Chapter 5 for more information about these forms of adapting information.) In each case, the specific information chosen and the way it is adapted will depend on the thesis and the writer's need to provide support, unity, and coherence to serve the thesis.

Attribution of information—The research paper writer must make explicitly clear which information was gathered from sources outside her/his own knowledge and experience and outside common knowledge. The writer must clearly identify the outside source used for this information.

Documentation of sources—The research paper writer must provide the reader with a detailed listing of the outside sources used in the paper. This listing must offer information that allows the reader to find and consult each of the sources used. This would include the author of the source, its title, how, where, and when it was published, and enough detail to locate the exact piece of information used.

Related Concepts

Style Guidelines—Different colleges and different programs within schools have their own preferred style guidelines for research papers, guidelines which determine the required manuscript format and the method of attributing and documenting secondary sources. The Modern Language Association (MLA), the American Psychological Association (APA), the

University of Chicago Press, the American Medical Association (AMA), and other organizations have all developed standardized guidelines for use by researchers.

Your instructor and librarian can help you identify which style guidelines you should use at your college or in your program. They can also suggest handbooks, pamphlets, or Web pages that explain the preferred style and give examples of how it is used.

You will need to use these guidelines in completing the research paper assignment below.

12.4 Exercise / Evaluate

Research Paper Assignment

This assignment gives you the opportunity to write a research paper. Keep in mind that a research paper is essentially an essay that relies for a substantial part of its evidence on sources other than the writer. Because you are already experienced with writing essays, you can focus your effort on incorporating your secondary research into your essay and on correctly attributing and documenting your sources.

The writing process will also guide you step by step as you complete this research paper.

Using the Writing Process

I. Before Writing

A. Getting Ideas

1. Choosing a topic—You may want to choose from among the topics mentioned above in the "Explore" activity, or from others acceptable to your professor. It helps to choose a topic that you find interesting or intriguing. A topic with which you are familiar but would like to know more about is a good start. You will have an opportunity to investigate or explore this topic in more detail.

2. Getting Ideas from Yourself—Free writing: Write for 15 minutes about your chosen topic. Put on paper everything you know about the topic. Keep in mind that free writing means writing without stopping to worry about ideas, organization, sentence structure, word use, or punctuation. If after 15 minutes you still have a lot to write, continue until you have completed transferring your knowledge to paper. Using what you already know will help direct your research. It will also help you avoid falling into plagiarism.

3. From Others—Read your free writing to find where the gaps are in your knowledge of the topic. Conduct research to find information to fill these gaps. Use the "Research Source Guide" above to help you use a variety of sources and to help you gather attribution and documentation details. In taking notes, be sure to keep track of whether you have collected a quote, paraphrase,

summary, or just individual details. Focus on gathering details. Use quotes and paraphrases only occasionally. Use summaries to get at the essence of lengthy sources.

II. During Writing

A. Planning

1. Establishing the Writing Context

Based on your own knowledge and the research you have gathered so far, decide upon the appropriate writing context for this research paper.

Who is the audience?

What form will be used?

When and where will it be set?

What is the purpose of the paper?

What process will be used?

What sources will provide the majority of the evidence?

2. Formulating the Main Idea

You began with a general topic. Now it is important that you provide a focus to the topic to limit it to a manageable size and to make it more specific. Put your topic and focus together into a preliminary thesis statement.

3. Developing Support

With your preliminary thesis statement as a guide, gather together the objective and subjective evidence that you plan to use in your research paper. If you find gaps in your evidence, or if it seems to rely too heavily on subjective, second-hand, or biased sources, conduct additional research to further develop support for your thesis statement.

4. Organizing

Use the "Research Paper Template" below to organize what you have gathered so far.

Research Paper Template

Your name: _____   Audience: _____

Professor's name: _____   Purpose: _____

Course name: _____   Form: _____

Date: _____   Main Sources: _____

Title: _____

Introduction

Invitation (complete sentence):

Orientation (notes; include information about why the intended audience would be interested in this general topic):

Thesis statement (complete sentence; include a clear indication of which rhetorical form you will use in developing your paper):

Body

First Subtopic—Topic sentence (complete sentence):

Firm evidence (notes)   Soft evidence (notes)

Second Subtopic—Topic sentence (complete sentence):

Firm evidence (notes)   Soft evidence (notes)

Third Subtopic—Topic sentence (complete sentence):

Firm evidence (notes)   Soft evidence (notes)

Repeat as needed for additional subtopics:

Conclusion

Transition (word, phrase, or none):

Restatement of thesis statement (complete sentence):

Summary of main points (notes):

Final thought (complete sentence):

Initial Impression

Strengths of the research paper:

Weaknesses of the research paper:

Actions needed to address weaknesses:

II. During Writing (continued)

D. Writing

Use the writing strategy that you believe will work best for this essay. You can use One Step after Another, Body First, Outside In, Microcosm, Whatever Works, or another strategy of your own or someone else's design.

III. After Writing

A. Reviewing

<u>1. Self-Review</u>

Use the "Responding to a First Draft" sheet and the "Review/Evaluation Guide" to help you make improvements to your first draft before sharing it with someone else.

<u>2. Expert Review</u>

Because incorporating secondary research into an essay and correctly attributing and documenting sources is quite challenging, it is especially important that you receive detailed feedback from an expert on this research paper. Even before sharing the paper with your instructor, you may want to seek out feedback from writing tutors available on your campus.

B. Finishing

<u>Rewrite</u> as needed, using feedback from the review step. You will need to carefully check your quotes, paraphrases, summaries, and individual details to assure that they accurately represent the original and are correctly attributed and documented. If you identify a problem, you may need to return to the original source for clarification. If you cannot resolve the problem, you may need to delete the material in question to avoid inaccuracy or plagiarism.

<u>Proofread</u> carefully to assure that you have followed the style guidelines correctly and that you have not overlooked any mistakes.

C. Sharing/Publishing

After you have finished your research paper, you should share it with the intended audience.

12.5 Extend

Beyond the Classroom—Now it is time to celebrate all the hard work you put into developing your writing skills.

Extras

Quick Reference

The Writing Process

I. Before Writing

A. Getting Ideas

    1. From Yourself
        a. Knowledge
            Analyzing
            Brainstorming
            Combining
            Free Writing
            Listing
            Questioning

        b. Experience
            Describing
            Journaling
            Observing

    2. From Others
        a. Primary Research
            Corresponding
            Discussing
            Interviewing
            Surveying
            Experimenting

        b. Secondary Reseach
            Listening
            Reading
            Watching

B. Grouping Ideas

    1. Chronology
    2. Sequence
    3. Classification
    4. General to Specific, or Specific to General
    5. Most to Least, or Least to Most

II. During Writing

A. Planning

1. Establishing the Writing Context
   a. Audience
   b. Purpose
   c. Form
   d. Setting
   e. Source
   >   Self
   >   Others

2. Formulating a Main Idea
   a. Topic
   b. Focus
   >   Time
   >   Place
   >   Number or Sequence
   >   Category or Characteristic
   >   Similarity or Difference
   >   Quality
   >   Cause or Effect
   >   Problem or Solution

3. Developing Support
   a. Objective Evidence
   >   Facts and Statistics
   >   Observations
   >   Records
   >   Expert Testimony

   b. Subjective Evidence
   >   Precedent
   >   Analogies
   >   Experience
   >   Opinion

4. Organizing
   a. Outlining
   >   Basic Outline
   >   Sentence Outline

   b. Paragraphing

   c. Using Essay Structure

B. Writing

1. One Step after Another
2. Body First
3. Outside In
4. Microcosm
5. Whatever Works

III. After Writing

A. Reviewing

1. Self-Review
2. Peer Review
3. Expert/Mentor Review

B. Rewriting

C. Proofreading

D. Sharing or Publishing

The Writing Context

Audiences for Writing

General readers—This includes everybody.

Specific groups—This includes only those people who have certain characteristics.

Experts—These are people who have a lot of knowledge of and experience with specific topics.

Your peers—These are people with whom you have many characteristics in common.

One person—This is one specific person.

Yourself—This is you.

Purposes for Writing

To Share or Express

To Inform or Explain

To Prove or Persuade

Rhetorical Forms

Narration—Telling a story from beginning to end.

Process—Explaining step by step how something is done.

Classification and Division—Taking many things and grouping them together by type, or taking one thing and dividing it into its parts.

Description—Describing the characteristics of a subject.

Comparison and Contrast—Focusing on the similarities and/or differences of two or more subjects.

Evaluation—Judging a subject against a set of established standards or criteria.

Cause and Effect—Following how some events lead to others.

Problem and Solution—Identifying and defining an issue and offering ways to address it.

Main Ideas

An effective topic sentence or thesis statement:

1. Needs a topic (general idea, question, or problem to be explored) and the focus that limits the topic. Focusing tools (specific aspects) include:

> time
> place
> number or sequence
> category or characteristic
> similarity or difference
> quality (good, bad, or other)
> cause or effect
> problem or solution

2. Places the topic in the subject position of the sentence. For this reason, a strong topic sentence does not begin with "There is/are" or "It is/They are."

3. Is a statement (a never question) that requires further development. It is not an obvious statement that can be completely explained in a single sentence.

Developing Support

Firmer Evidence	Softer Evidence

objective evidence:
    facts and statistics—information proven through repeated examination and analysis.
    observations—things that you or others have noted and that can be confirmed.
    records—historical information written down or stored.
    expert testimony—the judgment of someone who specializes in the topic.
	subjective evidence:
	    precedent—something should be because it was done before.
	    analogies—something is _____ because it is like something else that is _____.
	    experience—something is _____ because it happened to you or others.
	    opinion—judgment based on personal views and beliefs.

first-hand evidence—evidence that is direct from the source	**second-hand evidence**—indirect evidence reported by other than the original source
evidence that is unbiased—evidence provided by a source that has no interest or gain related to the evidence	**evidence that is biased**—evidence provided by a source that has interest or gain related to the evidence

Organizing

Outlining

See the organizing templates below.

Essay Template, page 197.

Sentence Outline, page 199.

Paragraph Structure

1. Topic Sentence = Topic (as subject of the sentence) + Focus

   - time
   - place
   - number or sequence
   - category or characteristic
   - similarity or difference
   - quality (good, bad, or other)
   - problem or solution
   - cause or effect

2. Clarifying Sentence

   - restatement
   - explanation
   - analogy

3. Support—Firm evidence and/or Soft evidence. All evidence demonstrates

   - logical development
   - unity
   - coherence

4. Concluding Statement—Connects to

   - topic sentence
   - the next subtopic, and/or
   - the thesis of the essay

Essay Structure

Topic _____

I. Introduction

A. Invitation—attracts attention and sparks interest in the thesis

<u>Types of Invitations</u>
A quotation
A question
A surprising comment
A brief definition
A general statement of fact
An explanation of the topic's importance
An explanation of the topic's timeliness
An appeal to common experience
An anecdote—a brief story related to the topic

B. Orientation—a few to several sentences that provide background information on the thesis or connects the thesis to the reader's experience

C. Proposition—what the essay is going to be about
Thesis statement—idea that the writer will explore and develop with evidence
Preview—one or two sentences that clarify a complicated thesis and provide the reader a look at the subtopics that will be covered in the body

II. Body Paragraph
(See Paragraph Structure above.)

III. Conclusion

A. Transition—a transition word, phrase, or sentence to let the reader know that the body has been completed and the essay is soon to end

B. Reflection:
Review—a summary of the ideas developed in the body
Restatement—the thesis in different words

C. Resolution—a sentence or two that reorients readers to the world, a final thought that leaves readers with a feeling that they have been informed, entertained, inspired, or persuaded

Organizing Templates

Essay Template

Your name: _____   Audience: _____

Professor's name: _____   Purpose: _____

Course name: _____   Essay type: _____

Date: _____   Source: _____

Title: _____

Introduction

Invitation (complete sentence):

Orientation (notes; include information about why the intended audience would be interested in this general topic):

Thesis statement (complete sentence; include a clear indication that the essay is a comparison):

Body

First Subtopic—Topic sentence (complete sentence):

<u>Firm evidence (notes)</u>   <u>Soft evidence (notes)</u>

Second Subtopic—Topic sentence (complete sentence):

<u>Firm evidence (notes)</u>   <u>Soft evidence (notes)</u>

Other Subtopic—Topic sentence (complete sentence):

Firm evidence (notes)	Soft evidence (notes)

Conclusion

Transition (word, phrase, or none):

Restatement of thesis statement (complete sentence):

Summary of main points (notes):

Final thought (complete sentence):

Initial Self-Review

Strengths of the essay:

Weaknesses of the essay:

Actions needed to address weaknesses:

Sentence Outline

Your name: _____   Audience: _____

Professor's name: _____   Purpose: _____

Course name: _____   Essay type: _____

Date: _____   Source: _____

Title: _____

I. Introduction

A. Write your invitation here. Write a complete sentence.

(What type of invitation did you choose? A quotation, a question, a surprising comment, a brief definition, a general statement of fact, an explanation of the topic's importance, an explanation of the topic's timeliness, an appeal to common experience, an anecdote—a brief story related to the topic)

B. What background information (history, news story, interesting fact, statistics, other), if any, should your reader have as orientation to the topic? Describe that information here in one sentence.

C. What is your thesis? Write a complete sentence here. Remember: (1) use focusing tools to clarify the topic of the essay; (2) make the topic of your essay the subject of your sentence; (3) be specific but not too specific; (4) include a preview of your subtopics in the order that you will develop them.

II. Body

A. Do you need to include an extended background section here? What information will this section contain. Summarize your ideas in one sentence.

B. Write the topic sentence for your 1st subtopic here. Write a complete sentence. Use coherence techniques to link this subtopic to your thesis.

1.   What objective evidence will you use to develop this subtopic? Summarize in one complete sentence the facts, statistics, expert testimony, observations, and/or records that you will use.

2.   What subjective evidence will you use to develop this subtopic? Summarize in one complete sentence the analogies, precedents, opinions, and/or experience that you will use.

C.   Write the topic sentence for your 2nd subtopic here. Write a complete sentence. Use coherence techniques to link this subtopic to your thesis.

1.   What objective evidence will you use to develop this subtopic? Summarize in one complete sentence the facts, statistics, expert testimony, observations, and/or records that you will use.

2.   What subjective evidence will you use to develop this subtopic? Summarize in one complete sentence the analogies, precedents, opinions, and/or experience that you will use.

3.   Repeat 1 and 2 for additional subtopics, if needed.

III. Conclusion

A. What kind of transition will you use to help the reader go from the body to the conclusion?

B. What has the reader learned about your topic? Restate your thesis in new words. Write one complete sentence here.

C. Write a summary of your subtopics in one complete sentence here.

D. Give your reader something to think about as s/he leaves your paper. Write a resolution or final thought here. Make it a complete sentence. What type of resolution will you use? (What type of invitation did you choose? A quotation, a question, a surprising comment, a brief definition, a general statement of fact, an explanation of the topic's importance, an explanation of the topic's timeliness, an appeal to common experience, an anecdote—a brief story related to the topic)

Review Sheets

Quick Self-Review Sheet

Your name: _____   Audience: _____

Professor's name: _____   Purpose: _____

Course name: _____   Essay type:_____

Date: _____   Source: _____

Title: _____

Answer the following questions with Yes or No. If you answer No, make the additions or changes necessary to answer Yes.

General

1. Does the essay have a title?

2. Is the audience for the essay clear?

3. Is the purpose for the essay clear?

4. Does the essay describe a process (a sequence of steps)?

Introduction

5. Does the essay have an introductory paragraph?

6. Does the essay have an invitation to attract the interest of the audience?

7. Does the essay have a thesis statement, one complete sentence that clearly states the main idea?

8. Does the thesis statement focus on a specific idea?

Body

9. Are the points that support the thesis developed in detail?

10. Do the supporting points clearly connect with the thesis?

11. Are there enough supporting points?

12. Does the body of the essay include firm evidence?

13. Is the evidence adequate to convince the readers?

Conclusion

14. Is there a concluding paragraph?

15. Does the conclusion include at least one: a restatement of the thesis; a summary of the main points; a call to action?

16. Does the paper give a feeling of completeness?

Sentence Structure, Word Use, and Punctuation

17. Have you carefully checked the grammar and vocabulary to avoid as many mistakes as possible?

Plan for Second Draft

18. What questions need to be answered before the next draft? What changes need to be made?

Responding to a First Draft

Answer the following questions with as much detail as you can. Answering these questions will require you to show that you understand what is being done in the paper.

General

1. What is the title? It should give an idea of the main idea of the paper.

2. Who is the main intended audience? Who should read this essay? Check one.
_____General readers   _____Specific groups   _____Experts
_____The writer's peers   _____One specific person   _____The writer her/himself

3. What is the main purpose? (check one)
_____Share or Express   _____Inform or Explain   _____Prove or Persuade

4. What form is used primarily? (check one)
___Narrative   ___Process   ___Classification and Division
___Description   ___Comparison and Contrast   ___Evaluation
___Cause and Effect   ___Problem and Solution

Introduction

5. Does the paper have an introductory paragraph? If not, how is the reader oriented to the information presented?

6. The Invitation. How is the reader's interest in this paper attracted? (check one)
___a funny story   ___a difficult question   ___a famous quotation
___a challenge   ___a similar or different experience ___something new
___something old in a new light   ___a statement of general interest

7. What is the thesis statement? (main idea sentence)

8. How was the general topic focused? (Check all that apply.)
___time   ___place   ___number or sequence   ___category or characteristic
___similarity/difference   ___quality   ___cause/effect   ___problem/solution

Body

9. What are the 3 to 5 main points developed in the body of the paper?

10. Do they support the thesis statement? How?

11. Are there points that could be added or removed? What are they?

12. What forms of evidence have been used? (Check all that apply.)
___facts and statistics   ___observations   ___records   ___expert testimony
___precedents   ___analogies   ___experience   ___opinions

13. Is the evidence adequate to convince the readers? If not, what should be done?

Conclusion

14. Is there a concluding paragraph? If not, how is the reader reminded of the key points?

15. Which of the following is included in the conclusion? (Check all that apply.)
_____a restatement of thesis   _____a summary of main points
_____a famous quotation related to thesis   _____a call to action

16. Does the paper give a feeling of completeness? If not, what is missing, and what should be done?

Sentence Structure, Word Use, and Punctuation

17. Carefully check each of the following items to assure that as many mistakes as possible have been corrected.

___complete sentences   ___appropriate verb tenses   ___uses transitions
___subject/verb agreement   ___correct word forms   ___spelling
___correct word order   ___capitals and full stops   ___format
___modifiers correctly located

Plan for Second Draft

18. What questions need to be answered before the next draft? What changes need to be made?

Review/Evaluation Guide

I—Ideas and Information
1. Is the main idea of the writing clear (topic and focus)?
2. Does the evidence provided relate to the thesis of the essay and/or the topic of the paragraph (unity)?
3. Is the objective evidence adequate to meet the requirements of the writing context?
4. If used, is the subjective evidence appropriate to the writing context?
5. Are the ideas and information presented accurate and reliable? and correctly attributed?

O—Organization
1. Does the organization of the writing follow the guidelines for an essay or other type of writing?
2. Is the organization appropriate to the rhetorical form(s) used?
3. Are paragraphs organized according to appropriate guidelines?
4. Does the organization (both essay and paragraph) support the logical development of the thesis?
5. Are transitions and repetition used effectively to link the elements of the writing (coherence)?

S—Sentence Structure
1. Are all of the sentences complete? Are simple, compound, and complex sentences correctly structured?
2. Are the verb tenses appropriate?
3. Do all subjects and verbs agree in number? Do all nouns and pronouns agree in number and gender?
4. Are modifiers appropriately linked to the words they modify?
5. Do words, phrases, and clauses follow the guidelines for sentence order and parallelism?

W—Word Use
1. Are the correct content words used?
2. Are the correct word forms used?
3. Are the words used appropriate to the writing context in terms of register, formality, and level of specificity?
4. Are the correct function words used?
5. Are all words spelled correctly?

P—Punctuation Plus
1. Is the manuscript format appropriate to the writing context?
2. Does the paper meet any required style guidelines?
3. Are sections (if used) and paragraphs set off appropriately (indenting and spacing)?
4. Is sentence punctuation correct? Are full stops (. ? !), dividers (, ; : — ( )), and others (" " ...) used correctly?
5. Is word punctuation correct? Are apostrophes, hyphens, capital letters, italics, abbreviations, and numbers used correctly?

Proofreading Help

Sentence Structure

Simple Sentence

Subject + Verb (with time).   (only 1 subject and 1 verb)

Compound Sentence

Subject + Verb (with time) + **coordinating conjunction** + Subject + Verb (with time).
(independent clause)

and	but
for	nor
or	so
yet	

(independent clause)

(Use a comma between the first independent clause and the coordinating conjunction when the clause is more than 5-7 words.)

Complex Sentence

Subject + Verb (with time) + **subordinating conjunction** + Subject + Verb (with time).
(independent clause)   (dependent clause)

OR

Subordinating conjunction + Subject + Verb (with time), + Subject + Verb (with time).
(dependent clause)   (independent clause)

Subordinating conjunctions include:

TIME

after	as	as soon as	before	by the time that
since	until	when	whenever	while

CAUSE and EFFECT

because	in order that	since (= because)	so that

CONTRAST

although	even though	though	whereas	while (=whereas)

CONDITION

even if	if	in the event that	provided that
unless	whether or not		

Word Use

Verb Endings

The following word endings are often, but not always, a signal that the word is a verb. (English often uses words in more than one role. That means that a verb may also be used as another word form—noun, adjective, or adverb—without changing. Also, words evolve in English, changing form and meaning over time.)

But, if you see these endings, you can take them as one clue that the word is a verb. You can use the other clues you learned about verbs to confirm that the word is, in fact, a verb in a particular context.

Simple Form (Infinitive) Endings

-ace	-act	-ade	-age	-ail
-aim	-ain	-ake	-ape	-are
-ase	-ate	-ave	-aze	-bble
-cede	-ceive	-ddle	-each	-ear
-ease	-eat	-ect	-en	-end
-esce	-ess	-ete	-fer	-ffle
-ggle	-ght	-ibe	-ice	-ict
-ide	-ieve	-ify	-ign	-ind
-ine	-ing	-ink	-ire	-ise
-iss	-ite	-ive	-ize	-join
-mble	-mit	-ngle	-ode	-oke
-olve	-ore	-ose	-ounce	-ound
-ove	-ssle	-tch	-the	-ttle
-uce	-uct	-ude	-ume	-ure
-use	-ute	-ven	-verse	-vert
-vest	-view	-zzle		

Tense/Aspect Endings

-ing	-ed	-en

Irregular Verbs

arise	arose	arisen	arising
bear	bore	born	bearing
beget	begat	begotten	begetting
begin	began	begun	beginning
bend	bent	bent	bending
bind	bound	bound	binding
bite	bit	bitten	biting
bleed	bled	bled	bleeding
break	broke	broken	breaking
bring	brought	brought	bringing
broudcast	broadcast	broadcast	broadcasting
build	built	built	building
buy	bought	bought	buying
cast	cast	cast	casting
catch	caught	caught	catching
cling	clung	clung	clinging
come	came	come	coming
cut	cut	cut	cutting
deal	dealt	dealt	dealing
dig	dug	dug	digging
dive	dove	divcd	diving
do	did	done	doing
draw	drew	drawn	drawing
drink	drank	drunk	drinking
drive	drove	driven	driving
drown	drown	drown	drowning
eat	ate	eaten	eating
fall	fell	fallen	falling
feed	fed	fed	feeding
feel	felt	felt	feeling
fight	fought	fought	fighting
find	found	found	finding
fit	fit	fit	fitting
fling	flung	flung	flinging
fly	flew	flown	flying
forbid	forbade	forbidden	forbidding
forget	forgot	forgotten	forgetting

give	gave	given	giving
go	went	gone	going
grind	ground	ground	grinding
grow	grew	grown	growing
hang	hung	hung	hanging
have	had	had	having
hear	heard	heard	hearing
hide	hid	hidden	hiding
hit	hit	hit	hitting
hold	held	held	holding
hurt	hurt	hurt	hurting
keep	kept	kept	keeping
kneel	knelt	knelt	kneeling
know	knew	known	knowing
lay	laid	laid	laying
lead	led	led	leading
leave	left	left	leaving
lend	lent	lent	lending
lie	lay	lain	lying
light	lit	lit	lighting
make	made	made	making
meet	met	met	meeting
outdo	outdid	outdone	outdoing
pay	paid	paid	paying
quit	quit	quit	quitting
read	read	read	reading
rid	rid	rid	ridding
ride	rode	ridden	riding
ring	rang	rung	ringing
run	run	run	running
say	said	said	saying
seek	sought	sought	seeking
sell	sold	sold	selling
send	sent	sent	sending
set	set	set	setting
shake	shook	shaken	shaking
shrink	shrunk	shrunk	shrinking
shut	shut	shut	shutting
sing	sang	sung	singing
sit	sat	sat	sitting

sleep	slept	slept	sleeping
slide	slid	slid	sliding
slit	slit	slit	slitting
speak	spoke	spoken	speaking
spend	spent	spent	spending
split	split	split	splitting
spread	spread	spread	spreading
stand	stood	stood	standing
steal	stole	stole	stealing
stick	stuck	stuck	sticking
sting	stung	stung	stinging
stink	stunk	stunk	stinking
strike	struck	struck	striking
swear	swore	sworn	swearing
swim	swam	swum	swimming
swing	swung	swung	swinging
take	took	taken	taking
teach	taught	taught	teaching
tear	tore	torn	tearing
tell	told	told	telling
think	thought	thought	thinking
throw	threw	thrown	throwing
underlie	underlay	underlain	underlying
understand	understood	understood	understanding
upset	upset	upset	upsetting
wake	woke	wakcd	waking
wear	worn	worn	wearing
weave	wove	woven	weaving
weep	wept	wept	weeping
win	won	won	winning
wind	wound	wound	winding
withdraw	withdrawn	withdrawn	withdrawing
wring	wrung	wrung	wringing
write	wrote	written	writing

Noun Endings

The following word endings are often, but not always, a signal that the word is a noun.

(English often uses words in more than one role. That means that a noun may also be used as another word form—verb, adjective, or adverb—without changing. Also, words evolve in English, changing form and meaning over time.)

But, if you see these endings, you can take them as one clue that the word is a noun. You can use the other clues you learned about nouns to confirm that the word is, in fact, a noun in a particular context.

General Noun Endings

-ac	-acy	-age	-an	-ance
-ancy	-ant	-ary	-ate	-cle
-cule	-dom	-ee	-eer	-ence
-ency	-er	-ess	-ette	-hood
-ia	-ic	-ics	-ier	-ion
-ism	-ist	-ity	-ive	-let
-ment	-mony	-ness	-nym	-or
-ry	-ship	-sis	-ster	-tude
-ty	-ule	-ure	-us	-y

Plural Endings

Regular
-s	-es

Irregular
-a	-en	-i

Possessive Nouns

-'s (singular)	-s' (plural)

Adjective and Adverb Endings

The following word endings are often, but not always, a signal that the word is either an adjective or adverb.

(English often uses words in more than one role. That means that an adjective or adverb may also be used as another word form—noun, verb, adjective, or adverb—without changing. Also, words evolve in English, changing form and meaning over time.)

But, if you see these endings, you can take them as one clue that the word is an adjective or adverb. You can use the other clues you learned about nouns to confirm that the word is, in fact, an adjective or adverb in a particular context.

General Adjective Endings

-able	-aceous	-acious	-al	-an
-ar	-ary	-ate	-ble	-ed
-ent	-ful	-ible	-ic	-ical
-id`	-ile	-ine	-ish	-ive
-less	-ory	-ose	-ous	

General Adverb Endings

-ly	-ward	-wisc

Prepositions

about	above	across	after
against	along	among	around
at	before	behind	below
beneath	between	beyond	by
concerning	down	during	except
for	from	in	into
near	of	off	on
onto	over	past	since
through	till	to	toward
under	until	upon	with

Index

A

action verbs, 7
adjective clauses, 89, 91–96, 98, 110–113
adjective phrases, 9, 89–90, 111, 113–114
adjectives, 6–7, 9, 14, 17, 33, 37, 59, 88, 90–91, 95–96, 98, 109–110, 113, 115, 135–137, 152–153, 155, 208, 212–213
adverbs, 6–9, 13–14, 17, 208, 212–213
almanac, 3, 17, 72, 85, 180–181
alphabet, 1, 4
analogy, 46, 48, 73, 103, 125, 127–128, 143, 147, 173–174, 176, 191, 194–195, 200–201, 205
analysis, 46, 53, 67, 130, 132, 134, 140–141, 143, 145, 155, 190, 194
appositives, 111
attribution, 58–59, 184–185
audience, 23, 26, 35, 41, 56, 70–71, 73, 75–76, 80–81, 99–100, 102, 104, 108, 117, 120–121, 124, 126–127, 140–142, 145–146, 155, 157, 160–161, 171–172, 175, 177, 186, 189, 191, 193, 197, 199, 202, 204
autobiography, 29

B

biased evidence, 46, 151, 186, 194
biography, 29–30
block-by-block organization, 108–109, 118–121, 123, 127
body, 49, 51, 56–58, 62–63, 74, 82, 101, 103, 108, 125, 144–145, 147, 155, 159, 174, 176, 196, 201, 203, 205
body first, 74, 175, 189, 192
brainstorming, 65, 68, 150, 190
building blocks, 4–11, 20

C

causative verbs, 167–168
cause (focus on), 165–167. *See also* effect
cause and effect, 11, 22, 102, 124, 146, 162–178, 193, 204, 207
cause and effect chain, 166
charts, 69–70, 180

chronology, 69, 75, 190
classification, 18–20, 22, 26–27, 69, 99, 102, 108, 124, 146, 175, 190, 193, 204
clause, 10–11, 33
clause markers, 33, 59, 91–95, 110–111, 113, 166
coherence, 21–23, 26–27, 48–49, 52, 63, 101, 123, 143, 145, 159, 173, 174, 184, 195, 200, 206
coincidence, 162–163, 177–178
combining sentences, 91–95, 97, 113
common nouns, 8, 87
comparatives, 14, 109–110, 115, 136
comparison, 22, 106–128, 140, 193, 204
complete sentence, 10–12, 16, 33, 81, 92–95, 103, 123, 125, 141–144, 147, 153, 167, 177, 206
conclusion, 22, 48, 56–58, 61–62, 74–75, 82, 101, 103, 122, 125, 144–145, 147, 158, 174, 176–177, 188, 196, 198, 201, 203, 205
consonants, 5–6
content words, 6–9, 17, 206
continuants, 5
contrast, 11, 22, 106–128, 140, 193, 204, 207
correlation, 162–163, 167, 169, 178
corresponding, 68, 190
count nouns, 8
criteria, 22, 129, 134, 137–138, 140, 149, 151, 193

D

deceptive practices, 64
decision making, 149
deduction, 53
dependent clause, 11, 33, 207
description, 22, 48, 84–105, 108–110, 116, 130, 135, 193, 204
descriptive words, 86–89
determiners, 9, 89–90, 96
development, 10, 18–27, 48–50, 57, 73, 101, 123, 159, 194–195, 206

diagrams, *See* charts
dictionary, 10, 72, 96
direct quote, 58, 60
discussing, 68, 190
division, 22, 26, 193, 204. *See also* classification
documentation, 184–186

E

effect (focus on), 165–167. *See also* cause
encyclopedia, 3, 27, 29, 72, 85, 105, 180–181
essay development, 44–64
evaluation, 9, 22, 27, 63, 83, 88, 90, 96, 105, 127, 129–149, 151, 159, 184, 193, 204, 206
evaluation words, 135–137
evidence, 21, 44–46, 49–49, 53, 57, 64, 68, 73, 82, 100, 103, 107, 117, 125, 134, 140, 143, 145, 147, 149, 155, 159, 163, 171–178, 184–188, 191, 194–206
experience, 30, 35, 41, 46, 53, 56–57, 63, 65, 68, 71, 73, 138, 142–144, 162, 183–185, 190–191, 193–196, 199–201, 204–205
expert testimony, 46, 73, 103, 143, 172–176, 191, 194, 200–201, 205
exposition, 53

F

facts, 46, 72–73, 103, 143, 149, 172, 191, 194, 200–201, 205
false analogy, 127
false causes, 178
famous quotations, 55, 102–103, 204–205
first-hand evidence, 46, 194
focus, 21–22, 24–27, 48, 63, 72, 81, 102, 108–110, 141–142, 159, 165, 191, 193–195, 199, 202, 204, 206
form, *See* patterns of development
free writing, 68, 117–118, 185, 190
full stops, 27, 103, 160, 205–206
function words, 6, 9, 11, 206

I–J

independent clause, 11, 33, 167, 207
induction, 53
interview, 43, 68, 171, 183, 190
introduction, 56–57, 61–63, 74–75, 80–81, 101–102, 121, 124, 142, 157, 172, 187, 196–199, 202, 204
invitation, 56–58, 61–62, 81, 101–102, 121, 124, 142, 146, 196–199, 201–204
journaling, 68, 190

L

level of sophistication, 71
listing, 68, 99, 190
logic, 21, 53, 134, 159, 195, 206
logical fallacies, 178

M

metaphors, 127–128
misplaced modifiers, 113–115
modal auxiliaries, 137
modifiers, 89–90, 103, 113–115, 205–206
mottos, 54

N

narration, *See* narrative
narrative, 22, 28–43, 53, 69, 85, 102, 193, 204
noncount nouns, 8
nouns, 6, 8–10, 14, 87–91, 96, 107, 109, 111–114, 140, 167, 206, 208, 212

O

objective evidence, 46, 73, 100, 143, 159, 191, 194, 200–210, 206
observations, 46, 53, 73, 86, 98–99, 103, 140, 143, 171–176, 191, 194, 200–201, 205
observing, 68, 134, 190
opinion, 46, 73, 103, 140, 143, 149, 173–174, 178, 191, 194, 200–201, 205
orientation, 57, 61–62, 101, 121, 130, 142, 157, 173, 187, 196–197, 199
outline, 49–53, 100, 118–120, 131–134, 141–144, 172, 191, 197–201
outside in, 74, 123, 159, 189, 192

P

paragraph, 18–27, 42, 48, 55–58, 70, 72, 74, 81–83, 159–160, 191, 195–196, 202–206
paraphrase, 59–60, 184–186, 189
patterns of development, 22, 193
periodicals, 29, 85, 180, 184
personal narrative, 30–31, 41
phonetic system, 4–5
phrases, 9
plagiarism, 179, 185, 189
point-by-point organization, 108–109, 118, 120–121, 123
precedent, 46, 73, 103, 143, 173–174, 191, 194, 200–201, 205
prepositional phrases, 9, 90–91, 96–98, 111–113
prepositions, 9, 31–32, 90–91, 166, 213
preview, 48, 57, 61–62, 142, 196, 199
primary research, 68, 140–141, 183, 190
problem solving, 151, 160–161
problem and solution, 150–161
processes, 66. *See also* writing process
proper nouns, 8, 87
proposition, 57, 61–62
punctuation, 12, 27, 58–60, 71, 75, 103–105, 160, 203–206
purpose, 70–73, 87, 100, 102, 120–121, 124, 178, 186–187, 191, 193, 197, 199, 202, 204

Q

questioning, 68, 90
quotation marks, 58
quotes, 58–61, 185–186, 189

R

records, 46, 73, 103, 125, 143, 172–176, 191, 194, 200–201, 205
reduced adjective clauses, 110–114
reference books, 3, 29–30, 55, 85, 127
reflection, 48, 57–58, 61–62, 196
register, 71, 160, 206
repetition, 22–23, 143, 159, 206
reported speech, 59–61

research, 43, 66, 68, 83, 140–141, 145, 148–149, 161, 171–172, 179–190
research paper, 22, 66, 179–189
resolution, 58, 61–62, 101, 144, 174, 196, 201
restatement, 57–58, 61–62, 82, 101, 103, 122, 125, 188, 195–196, 198, 203, 205
rhetorical forms, *See* patterns of development

S

second-hand evidence, 46, 194
secondary research, 68, 171–172, 184–185, 189
sentences, *See* complete sentence
sequence, 21, 24, 30, 69, 72, 75–81, 102, 162–163, 171, 178, 190–191, 194–195, 202, 204
setting, 70, 191
similes, 127–128
slogans, 54, 64
sound system, *See* phonetic system
sources, 3–4, 17, 70, 85, 132, 151, 161, 180–186, 189
standards, *See* criteria
statistics, *See* facts
stative verbs, 7, 112
stops, 5. *See also* full stops
style, 71, 75, 160, 177, 184–185, 189, 206
subject (grammatical), 10–11, 21, 33, 110–113, 125, 152, 160, 194–195, 199, 205–207
subjective evidence, 46, 73, 100, 143, 159, 173–174, 186, 191, 194, 200–201, 206
subjunctive, 152–153, 155, 160
summarizing, 22, 59, 184
summary, 48, 57–58, 82, 103, 122, 152, 155, 157, 186, 196, 198, 201, 203, 205
superlatives, 7, 9, 14, 136–137
support, 21–22, 25, 27, 48, 52, 56, 63–64, 73–74, 82, 101, 103, 125, 134, 156, 159, 184, 186, 191, 194–195, 203, 205–206
surveying, 68, 190
SWOT, 155–156
syllables, 5–6, 10, 14–15, 110, 136

T

thesaurus, 72, 96

thesis statement, 48, 57, 61–62, 72–74, 81, 100–103, 121, 124–125, 155, 186–188, 194, 196–198, 202, 204–205

time clauses, 31, 33

time focus, 6, 32–35

time frames, 6, 10–11, 31–35, 41, 70, 75–76

time phrases, 31

timelines, 69

tone (pronunciation), 6; (writing), 71

topic, 20–22, 24–25, 27, 48, 51, 55, 71–73, 102, 142–143, 159, 173–174, 180, 185–186, 194–195, 199–200, 206

topic sentence, 21–22, 25, 48, 72–74, 100, 121–122, 143, 157–158, 173–174, 187–188, 194–195, 197–198, 200

transition words, 22–23, 27, 57–58, 61–63, 75–76, 101, 103, 122, 143–144, 147, 159, 166–167, 174, 196, 198, 201, 205–206

U

unity, 21, 25, 27, 42, 48, 52, 101, 159, 184, 195, 206

V

verb tenses, 31, 33, 35, 42, 60, 83, 103, 159, 205–206

verbs, 6–7, 9–10, 17, 39, 41, 59–60, 77–80, 88, 98, 112, 117, 140, 152–153, 155, 160, 167–168, 206, 208–211

voiced sounds, 5

voiceless sounds, 5

vowel sounds, 4–6, 12–13

vowels, 4–5

W

webs, 70

word forms, 13, 59, 103, 160, 205–206, 208, 212–213

words, 6–10, 27, 113, 116, 128, 135, 160, 206, 208, 212–213

writing context, 70–72, 100, 120, 159–160, 186, 191, 193, 206

writing process, 67–75, 95, 117, 140, 155, 171, 185, 190–192

writing techniques, 73–74